THE BEDFORD SERIES IN HISTORY AND CULTURE

The Movements of the New Left, 1950–1975

A Brief History with Documents

Related Titles in
THE BEDFORD SERIES IN HISTORY AND CULTURE
Advisory Editors: Natalie Zemon Davis, *Princeton University*
Ernest R. May, *Harvard University*
Lynn Hunt, *University of California, Los Angeles*
David W. Blight, *Yale University*

THE BEDFORD SERIES IN HISTORY AND CULTURE

The Movements of the New Left, 1950–1975

A Brief History with Documents

Van Gosse

Franklin and Marshall College

BEDFORD/ST. MARTIN'S   Boston   ♦   New York

For Bedford/St. Martin's

Executive Editor for History: Mary V. Dougherty
Director of Development for History: Jane Knetzger
Developmental Editor: Ann Hofstra Grogg
Editorial Assistant: Carina Schoenberger
Senior Production Supervisor: Dennis J. Conroy
Production Associate: Chris Gross
Senior Marketing Manager: Jenna Bookin Barry
Project Management: Books By Design, Inc.
Text Design: Claire Seng-Niemoeller
Indexer: Books By Design, Inc.
Cover Design: Billy Boardman
*Cover Art: Central State University Protesters with Clenched Fists. Columbus, Ohio,
May 22, 1969.* © Bettmann/CORBIS
Composition: Stratford Publishing Services
Printing and Binding: Haddon Craftsmen, an RR Donnelley & Sons Company

President: Joan E. Feinberg
Editorial Director: Denise B. Wydra
Director of Marketing: Karen Melton Soeltz
Director of Editing, Design, and Production: Marcia Cohen
Manager, Publishing Services: Emily Berleth

Library of Congress Control Number: 2004107771

Manufactured in the United States of America.

0   9   8   7   6   5
f   e   d   c   b

For information, write: Bedford/St. Martin's, 75 Arlington Street, Boston, MA 02116
(617-399-4000)

ISBN: 0-312-13397-9 (paperback)
      1-4039-6804-7 (hardcover)
EAN: 978-0-312-13397-9

Acknowledgments

Acknowledgments and copyrights appear at the back of the book on pages 190–91,
which constitute an extension of the copyright page.

Foreword

The Bedford Series in History and Culture is designed so that readers can study the past as historians do.

The historian's first task is finding the evidence. Documents, letters, memoirs, interviews, pictures, movies, novels, or poems can provide facts and clues. Then the historian questions and compares the sources. There is more to do than in a courtroom, for hearsay evidence is welcome, and the historian is usually looking for answers beyond act and motive. Different views of an event may be as important as a single verdict. How a story is told may yield as much information as what it says.

Along the way the historian seeks help from other historians and perhaps from specialists in other disciplines. Finally, it is time to write, to decide on an interpretation and how to arrange the evidence for readers.

Each book in this series contains an important historical document or group of documents, each document a witness from the past and open to interpretation in different ways. The documents are combined with some element of historical narrative—an introduction or a biographical essay, for example—that provides students with an analysis of the primary source material and important background information about the world in which it was produced.

Each book in the series focuses on a specific topic within a specific historical period. Each provides a basis for lively thought and discussion about several aspects of the topic and the historian's role. Each is short enough (and inexpensive enough) to be a reasonable one-week assignment in a college course. Whether as classroom or personal reading, each book in the series provides firsthand experience of the challenge—and fun—of discovering, recreating, and interpreting the past.

Natalie Zemon Davis
Ernest R. May
Lynn Hunt
David W. Blight

Preface

The Movements of the New Left, 1950–1975, is a documentary history of New Left radicalism from its birth in the 1950s through its dispersion and institutionalization in the early 1970s. The book begins with the premise that to understand the multiple social movements of that period we have to recognize them collectively as the New Left. This conception departs from the commonplace definition of the New Left as the white student movement of the 1960s, placed between a civil rights movement beginning in the 1950s and the women's liberation movement cresting in the 1970s. An inclusive definition of the New Left is both more accurate and more useful in introducing students to the complex political dynamics of "the Sixties." Instead of learning about many separate strands of activism, students are encouraged to seek commonalities, to analyze how "the Movement" as a whole changed over time. In particular, I hope this book challenges students to think about the commitment shared by all of these movements to a radical understanding of democracy, and how that resonates in American history.

This book is therefore broad in coverage; no other collection of documents on the Sixties includes such a wide range of groups and individuals. In addition to the Student Nonviolent Coordinating Committee, Tom Hayden, Martin Luther King Jr., Betty Friedan, and Malcolm X, students will explore primary sources from the Mattachine Society, the Congressional Black Caucus, the Young Lords Party, Father Daniel Berrigan, and Congresswoman Bella Abzug. In addition to a wide variety of voices, students will encounter a broad range of source types, including manifestos, testimonies, speeches, newspaper advertisements, letters, and excerpts from books.

The organization of *The Movements of the New Left, 1950–1975,* combines chronological and thematic approaches. In the introduction to the documents each movement is examined in turn within a periodization of successive phases: first, the transition from the 1940s to the cold war era, when the first hints of a new radicalism appeared; second, the dramatic upsurge in 1960–65, as the civil rights movement peaked, creating space for other movements; third, the confrontation with cold war liberalism in 1965–68, led by the antiwar movement; finally, the culminating phase during Nixon's presidency, when many new movements emerged, and the larger Left dispersed.

The introduction is followed by forty-five documents, representing all parts of the New Left over a quarter century, from the earliest stirring of gay rights activism in 1950 through the consolidation of feminism and Black Power in the 1970s. Each document is introduced by a headnote that situates it historically and provides key information about its author. Footnotes clarify topical references within each document. The documents are followed by a chronology to help students trace the chain of causality between major events and various movements, questions for consideration to aid class discussion, and a selective bibliography for students who wish to pursue research on a particular movement or individual. Finally, the index lists all common acronyms—such as SNCC and SDS—for easy reference.

ACKNOWLEDGMENTS

I have incurred many debts in the nearly ten years it took to complete this book, from Charles Christensen, who originally signed it for the Bedford series in 1995, to Patricia Rossi, who oversaw its completion. I am grateful to both for encouraging the breadth of this work, and especially grateful to Patricia Rossi for her commitment to seeking out the best historical scholarship. At Bedford, I have benefited from the guidance of Ann Hofstra Grogg and Jane Knetzger. Their professionalism saved me from making many errors.

Among many helpful colleagues, I want to thank several who made documents available or read individual chapters. Max Elbaum shared with me his encyclopedic knowledge of the late sixties and the New Communist Movement. Lise Vogel encouraged me to rethink the conventional narrative of women's liberation. James Miller improved my understanding of Black Power, and is always a good friend. Jeffrey Escoffier pointed me at the right books to read on gay liberation. I owe a special debt to Ellen Schrecker, Yeshiva University, who originally inspired me to propose a Bedford book and has critiqued several versions of this manuscript. She and Nancy MacLean, Northwestern University; Robert O. Self, University of Wisconsin, Milwaukee; R. Warren Metcalf, University of Oklahoma; Peter B. Levy, York College; and John D'Emilio, University of Illinois at Chicago, were among the final group of readers who gave it a close reading and made it much better thereby. I thank all.

This book is dedicated to a fellow activist and historian, Johanna O'Mahony Gosse, and to her wonderful mother and fellow historian, Eliza Jane Reilly. They are my best teachers.

Van Gosse

Contents

APPENDIXES

THE BEDFORD SERIES IN HISTORY AND CULTURE

The Movements of the New Left, 1950–1975

A Brief History with Documents

PART ONE

Introduction:
A Movement
of Movements

Some historians characterize the New Left as a movement of young people seeking revolutionary change, one of many radical movements during the 1960s, such as Black Power, Women's Liberation, and the anti–Vietnam War movement. This book defines the New Left more broadly as the combination of all these movements, from civil rights in the 1950s to gay and women's rights in the 1970s. What linked these movements was the importance they placed on the dignity of each individual and the right of every American to full citizenship. This was a radically new vision of democracy, and it changed the United States in fundamental ways.

These movements began organizing in the early 1950s, when any kind of radical protest was very unpopular, but they did not attract widespread notice until the 1960s, when public protests and debates surged. Although the huge rallies and marches of the late 1960s lasted only a few years, many of the movements continued to grow in the 1970s and still play a role in the political arena today.

Consider, for example, the Mattachine Society, the first organization in U.S. history to campaign for the rights of gay people. It was founded in 1950 by Harry Hay, a young Los Angeles leftist and a gay man angered by police harassment. Hay was a member of the Communist Party, which championed equality for African Americans and

Latinos. Based on this experience, Hay developed his view of homosexuals as an "oppressed minority" capable of a "highly ethical homosexual culture" (see Document 1). He and a few others left the Communist Party to form the Mattachine Society. By 1953, however, other members of the society had pushed Hay out, worried that at the height of the anti-Communist campaign called the Red Scare, his left-wing background would cripple their efforts. A new radicalism was waiting to be born, but the struggle for gay civil rights would proceed cautiously.

The New Left had deep roots in the radical tradition that began with the American Revolution. Before the Civil War, abolitionists sought to extend the Revolution's promise of equality, refusing to accept the legitimacy of slavery and beginning the long campaign for women's suffrage. Then, from the 1880s through the 1940s, the Old Left of Socialists, Communists, and anarchists focused on the class struggle against industrial capitalism. After 1945, radicals returned to older questions about the limits of democracy. Were all people "created equal" with "inalienable rights," as the Declaration of Independence promised? If so, why were many Americans second-class citizens with few rights? This new focus on democracy for all included:

1. The right not to be segregated and despised because of your color
2. The right to vote and be represented by someone like yourself
3. The right to walk down the street unmolested, without fear of violence
4. The right to protest, without being labeled a subversive
5. The right to equal access to education, housing, and jobs, without regard to race or gender
6. The right to love whom you want, when you want, and how you want
7. The right to be left alone, to privacy and control over your own body

Today these demands may not seem very radical, but in the 1950s and 1960s, they represented a profound challenge to the established authority of white people, men, the government, and normative heterosexuality. To understand how revolutionary the New Left was, consider how much has changed since then. Today there are no COLORED and WHITE signs outside restaurants and bathrooms. It is illegal to deny someone a job because of his or her color or gender or religion. Federal, state, and local governments now include women and people of color in large numbers (although white men still predominate). Discrimination against gays has hardly ceased, but homosexuals participate in politics, adopt children, teach in schools, and lead religious congregations. Protests are an accepted part of political life. Some people still do see these changes as radical, and rejection of them has fueled a powerful New Right movement.

Besides their common commitment to extending democracy to all, the multiple movements of the New Left were linked in other fundamental ways as well. To a remarkable degree, they learned from one another, adapting similar strategies of confronting authority, exposing injustice, and provoking change. Two constantly repeated phrases capture the main strategies of the New Left: "speaking truth to power" and "the whole world is watching." The first was derived from the pacifist tradition of moral witness. It stressed the importance of confronting oppression nonviolently, even at personal risk. For the New Left, that meant "putting one's body on the line"—sitting in at segregated lunch counters, walking directly into police lines, lying down in front of trucks carrying nuclear weapons or trains carrying draftees bound for Vietnam, occupying buildings on college campuses, or disrupting speeches by government officials. The usual result of this strategy was arrest, often accompanied by beatings and incarceration for prolonged periods. Activists chose to participate in these protests because they knew that what they called "passive resistance," now usually described as civil disobedience, made oppression visible, a process greatly accelerated by the spread of new media technologies such as television, the instant transmittal of news photographs, and live radio broadcasting. As this book documents, the New Left consistently organized around the premise that the whole world was watching, and indeed it often was.

However naive or even risky these protest strategies appear to us now, they also were very practical. Confronted with activists willing to endure violence and unafraid of jail, authorities from the Deep South to university administrations to the White House lost political legitimacy. Violent repression, once taken for granted in some places, became odious when exposed to national and world public opinion. Protesters asserting their civil and human rights and standing on the U.S. Constitution claimed the moral high ground. Almost always reviled at first as "outside agitators" and publicity hounds, they eventually came to seem heroic as the unpopular truths they spoke became accepted by society at large.

SEEDS OF DISSENT IN THE 1940s AND 1950s

The New Left was a product of three historical developments that took place during and after World War II. These rapid shifts in the social and political landscape made radicalism seem treasonous but created the possibility of change.

First, World War II disrupted American society at every level, producing opportunities for many groups to challenge oppression. Tens of millions of Americans left farms, small towns, and urban neighborhoods to fight overseas or take defense positions. Millions of women and African Americans got high-paying, unionized factory jobs. As a result, civil rights agitation increased tenfold: How could America fight Nazism abroad and tolerate white supremacy at home? Native Americans and Latinos shared in this fight for rights, while Japanese Americans were put in concentration camps. Anonymous wartime life and same-sex environments fostered self-discovery by thousands of gay men and lesbians.

Second, soon after World War II, the cold war broke out between the United States and the Soviet Union. At home, the cold war led to the Red Scare. In the 1930s, Communists and other leftists helped build a powerful trade union movement, earning leadership positions. After 1945, however, organized labor became cautious, focusing its efforts on gaining higher wages and benefits for union members. Leftists lost their power base in the unions through internal expulsions. Radicals also were purged from universities, the entertainment industry, and the civil service. Thousands lost their jobs, and Communist leaders were jailed for advocating the government's overthrow. As activists were hauled before federal and state investigating committees (see Document 2), the Old Left lost its legitimacy.

Third, although the Red Scare affected all of American society by associating radicalism with subversion, it touched only a small number of people directly. In contrast, the postwar economic boom lifted millions of white working-class people into the middle class, enabling them to buy homes in the suburbs and send their children to college. What economist John Kenneth Galbraith dubbed the "affluent society" seemed to have banished poverty, and with it the class-based conflicts that energized the Old Left. Continued economic growth at home, combined with containing communism abroad, became the basis for the dominant political consensus that historians call cold war liberalism.

Cold war liberalism was a moderate ideology repudiating any taint of radicalism. In the 1930s, leftists supported President Franklin Delano Roosevelt's New Deal because its programs strengthened unions and helped working people. After World War II, however, the cold war shattered the liberal-left alliance, and Democratic liberals attacked the Old Left. In 1947, for example, Roosevelt's successor, Harry S. Truman, established loyalty boards to screen federal employees for subversive associations. Democrats such as Truman, Eleanor Roosevelt, John F. Kennedy, and Lyndon Johnson agreed with historian Arthur Schlesinger Jr. that liberalism should claim "the vital center" against both the right and the left.

Cold war liberals did have a vision of reform. They assumed no radical changes were needed, just better government programs. They supported aid for education and housing, gradual progress in civil rights, and aggressive military containment of communism abroad. They knew that the main threat to their control of government came not from the left, but from powerful right-wing groups that were hostile to any reform, including many southern Democrats. Republican conservatives, led by Wisconsin's Senator Joseph McCarthy, persistently charged Democrats with protecting Communist spies in the government. They advocated attacking the Soviet Union directly rather than just containing it. Anticommunism pervaded U.S. politics, providing a rationale for blocking all kinds of reform. For instance, segregationists in the South associated even moderate approaches to civil rights with communism. At first, the emerging New Left movements joined with cold war liberals against the reactionary right, hoping to enact real change. But later, as liberals escalated the Vietnam War, the New Left broke with them.

A radical revival began in the mid-1950s with the pent-up demand of black Americans for civil rights. For decades, black people had fought through the courts to overturn segregation. In twelve southern states they were denied the right to vote, relegated to unskilled jobs and miserable schools, and subjected to the threat of lynching. Although African Americans could vote in the North, conditions there were often little better than in the South, with de facto segregation the norm. During the 1940s, a civil rights alliance emerged among liberals, leftists, and trade unionists, both black and white. The Democratic

Party finally endorsed civil rights in 1948, when President Truman secured his reelection victory over Republican Thomas Dewey by desegregating the armed forces. Meanwhile, the National Association for the Advancement of Colored People (NAACP) won a series of legal battles, chipping away at segregation and disenfranchisement of African Americans. In Africa and Asia, nationalist movements challenged European colonialism, providing powerful evidence that white dominance was vulnerable. Finally, in the 1954 *Brown v. Board of Education* decision, the U.S. Supreme Court ruled that segregated schools were inherently unequal and unjust.

The *Brown* ruling invigorated civil rights activists but also led to the formation of White Citizens Councils throughout the South and a campaign dubbed "massive resistance" by southern white elites. The protest that would initiate a mass movement to topple Jim Crow (as the laws enforcing racial segregation were called) broke out in Montgomery, Alabama, when veteran NAACP activist Rosa Parks refused to give up her seat on a bus to a white man on December 1, 1955 (see Document 4). Her arrest set in motion a long-planned boycott of the city's bus system (see Document 3) that captured international attention. The boycott lasted more than a year, and in January 1957 the Supreme Court invalidated the bus segregation ordinance. The boycott's spokesman, a young Baptist minister named Martin Luther King Jr., became a nationally known figure. That January, he created a network of black ministers, the Southern Christian Leadership Conference (SCLC), which led dozens of civil rights campaigns in subsequent years. By combining Christian principles, nonviolence, and a conscious appeal to the U.S. Constitution, King and SCLC exposed the ugliness of segregation.

Still, in the late 1950s civil rights campaigns made little progress. Southern legislatures and governors refused to desegregate schools, denounced integration as a Communist plot, and tried to ban the NAACP. It became clear that only the federal government could enforce the law, but national leaders acted only under duress. In 1957, Arkansas Governor Orval Faubus used the National Guard to block black students from entering a high school in Little Rock after a federal judge had accepted an NAACP petition for desegregation. Reluctantly, President Dwight Eisenhower sent in U.S. Army troops to enforce the ruling, but that was a one-time event. The main question for civil rights activists became how to make the federal government take action to implement the law.

At the same time, a revived peace movement also contributed to the radical revival. Antimilitarism and pacifism had withered during and immediately after World War II, but the discovery that nuclear tests in the earth's atmosphere produced dangerous radioactive fallout spurred a new international peace movement led by scientists in the mid-1950s. In the United States, radical pacifists created the Committee for Non-Violent Action (CNVA) and *Liberation* magazine, which advocated a nonviolent, global revolution to end capitalism and war (see Document 5). It brought together liberals and socialists, blacks and whites, Marxists and religious people—anyone who opposed militarism and racism. It was the first magazine to publish the writings of Martin Luther King Jr. *Liberation*'s editorial stance was very influential in the early New Left. Resisting all forms of authoritarian rule, it argued for a "third way" outside the opposing camps of the two superpowers, the United States and the Soviet Union. Many of *Liberation*'s supporters also were active in the CNVA, which led protests against a possible nuclear holocaust by actions like symbolic blockades at Air Force bases. Moderate pacifists and liberals formed the Committee for a Sane Nuclear Policy (SANE). SANE focused on lobbying Congress and educating the public about nuclear testing as a first step toward disarmament. With the support of prominent citizens, it built a substantial membership (see Document 6).

Currents of cultural rebellion also fed into the New Left. The poets and writers known as the Beat Generation, like Allen Ginsberg and Jack Kerouac, became famous for rejecting the norms of middle-class society. New folk music and jazz subcultures on college campuses attracted rebellious young people, and even rock and roll, much more widely popular, revealed white youths' fascination with African American culture.

Another indication that some Americans might embrace radical change was the enthusiasm for Fidel Castro in Cuba. In 1957 and 1958, there was widespread sympathy for Castro's campaign to overthrow the U.S.-backed dictator, Fulgencio Batista. When Castro triumphed in January 1959, he was declared a liberator by the American media and toured the United States to great acclaim, although relations quickly soured.

THE MOVEMENTS TAKE OFF, 1960–1965

The first half of the 1960s is sometimes referred to nostalgically as the "good sixties," a time of idealism before the polarization of the late 1960s. Certainly, it was a period of prosperity and confidence in government, symbolized by the youthful administration of President John

F. Kennedy and the can-do Great Society proclaimed by his successor, Lyndon Johnson. The nation made major strides to overcome deeply rooted injustices, and the movements of the New Left, in alliance with liberals in the Democratic Party, played a central role.

The year 1960 was historic for both liberals and the New Left. That November, Kennedy beat the Republican presidential candidate, Vice President Richard Nixon, by a tiny margin. Both candidates were moderates, but young people were energized by Kennedy's pledge to "get the country moving" with programs such as the Peace Corps. That year also marked a breakthrough for the civil rights movement. On February 1, four black students at North Carolina Agricultural and Technical College in Greensboro sat in at a whites-only lunch counter in a Woolworth's department store, asking to be served and refusing to give up their seats until they were. Their nonviolent protest inspired sit-ins in dozens of cities across the South, thousands of arrests, and the formation of the Student Nonviolent Coordinating Committee (SNCC, pronounced "snick") in April 1960 (see Document 7). SNCC became one of the New Left's most influential organizations. Over the next five years, its young field secretaries pioneered a new strategy of grassroots community organizing in the Deep South's most dangerous counties. SNCC brought to national attention the voices of poor African Americans, such as Mississippi's Fannie Lou Hamer, whose courage inspired people of all races (see Document 10). Eventually, its commitment to "political power for poor black people" and "Freedom Now" led to Black Power.

Civil disobedience campaigns escalated steadily. In May 1961, the Congress of Racial Equality (CORE), an interracial pacifist group formed in 1942, organized Freedom Rides by teams of black and white activists who rode buses into the South to test the enforcement of desegregation statutes. They were met by organized violence in Alabama, where police permitted mobs to firebomb buses and physically attack Freedom Riders. Attorney General Robert Kennedy (the president's brother) stepped in, demanding that the state of Alabama protect the activists. Eventually, SNCC members took over from CORE and continued the rides into Mississippi, where dozens were jailed for months. International media coverage of this campaign embarrassed the Kennedy administration, demonstrating the extremes to which white supremacists, backed by conservative Democratic governors, would go to maintain segregation.

The following year, 1962, a federal court ordered the University of Mississippi to admit its first African American student, James Meredith. Hundreds of U.S. marshals sent to guarantee his safety were pinned down overnight by several thousand armed whites. It took troops from a nearby Air Force base to end the violence. Again, the Kennedys were embarrassed by open, violent defiance of the authority of the federal government.

During the Freedom Rides and subsequent civil rights campaigns, SNCC and CORE pursued a "jail no bail" strategy. This policy was intended to fill up prison cells and draw media attention to their cause. Established civil rights groups such as the NAACP were more cautious in their approach, seeking action through the courts and putting pressure on southern business leaders and other white moderates. Wishing to preserve their relationships with white labor, religious, and political leaders in the North, these groups were wary of radicalism. SCLC, led by King and other ministers, found itself in the middle. King was the undisputed leader of the movement because of his moral authority and renown. He was seen as the only one who could bring the civil rights establishment and the impatient younger generation together into a working coalition.

From 1960 to 1962, all the civil rights organizations struggled to find openings in the wall of "massive resistance," not only in the South but also in the North. SNCC began a voter registration project in rural Mississippi. SCLC ran voter registration schools throughout the South. CORE and the NAACP campaigned to desegregate public facilities and workplaces nationwide, from Oakland to Philadelphia. Victories were few, especially in the Deep South, where violence against African Americans was unrelenting. The Kennedy administration encouraged northern charitable foundations to set up the Voter Education Project to fund voter registration, so as to discourage high-profile campaigns such as the Freedom Rides. SNCC used its share of these funds to register voters in areas of the Deep South with overwhelming African American majorities but almost no black voters.

The civil rights movement crested between 1963 and 1965, mobilizing hundreds of thousands of African Americans to participate in demonstrations that forced the U.S. government to dismantle segregation. In April 1963, King and SCLC decided to confront white supremacy directly in Birmingham, Alabama, the South's industrial center and a city infamous for its violent racism. Knowing that Police Commissioner Eugene "Bull" Connor would not tolerate any kind of protest, King and other SCLC organizers sent hundreds of junior high school students into the downtown streets. As the television cameras rolled and the world watched, police knocked the students down with fire hoses, sicced dogs on them, and then hauled them off to jail. King also was arrested and from jail issued an urgent indictment of those who sought accommodation with racism (see Document 13). Increasingly, black protesters in Birmingham moved beyond nonviolence and showed a willingness to confront police and white mobs violently.

A settlement was finally reached in Birmingham, desegregating some public accommodations, but white resistance to civil rights increasingly dominated the domestic political agenda. Politicians like Alabama Governor George Wallace played to their all-white voter base, demanding "segregation now, segregation tomorrow, segregation forever." On June 11, President Kennedy spoke to the nation on live television, stressing the need to accept the civil rights revolution and to ensure that it was peaceful. He also promised to introduce a comprehensive civil rights bill in Congress. In the early hours of the next morning, Medgar Evers, the NAACP's field secretary in Mississippi, was assassinated in his driveway, indicating the volatility of the situation.

Later that summer, on August 28, 1963, a quarter of a million people gathered in Washington, D.C., for the March for Jobs and Freedom, the largest demonstration in U.S. history. The march was sponsored by six major civil rights organizations. At the Lincoln Memorial, King delivered his famous "I Have a Dream" speech. Afterward, he and others were invited to the White House to have tea with the president. But this historic event was marred by behind-the-scenes discord, as SNCC chairman John Lewis was forced to omit criticism of the president from his speech (see Document 14).

It was too soon to declare victory. Just weeks after the march, the Ku Klux Klan blew up Birmingham's oldest black Baptist church, killing four young girls. Although many thousands marched and went to jail, most African Americans in the South still lived under Jim Crow and only a minority could vote, while less visible segregation was pervasive in northern and western states. Among the millions who had migrated to northern cities in the decades since World War I, discontent was growing. Since World War II, both industries and middle-class whites had fled to the suburbs, and the living conditions of urban blacks were deteriorating. Although the civil rights movement was active in the North, seeking to end discrimination in employment, schools, and housing, it produced limited results. White northerners who attacked legalized segregation in the South supported a de facto version of it at home. In this context, African American radicals in cities such as Detroit and Oakland formed small groups that were the precursors of the Black Power movement. While few joined the Nation of Islam (NOI), a religious sect advocating complete separation from whites, many were inspired by one of its ministers, Malcolm X. With a slashing wit, he denounced nonviolence and alliances with white liberals, counseling African Americans that defeating white supremacy required a genuine revolution by any means necessary (see Document 15). In early 1964, Malcolm left the Nation of Islam and founded a new group, the Organization of Afro-American Unity, to press for black political and economic power. He visited Africa and the Middle East and declared that he no longer viewed all whites as enemies. In February 1965, he was killed by members of the NOI while speaking in Harlem.

In 1964 and 1965, ten years of black mobilization and white violence in the South forced Congress to finally pass bills outlawing segregation, racial discrimination, and disenfranchisement. These years seemed like a series of triumphs but they were mixed with disappointment, too, as for many black activists the victories came late and at great cost. In July 1964, Congress passed the Civil Rights Act, which received bipartisan support and banned discrimination based on race, ethnicity, and national origin in all public accommodations and employment (see Document 19). Now the focus shifted to voting rights.

Earlier that summer, SNCC built on years of community organizing in Mississippi to launch the Freedom Summer Project in alliance with CORE, SCLC, and the NAACP. Its goal was to register African American voters in the new Mississippi Freedom Democratic Party (MFDP), using the presence of white northerners to focus a national spotlight on the nation's most racist state. One thousand volunteers, mainly young whites, traveled to Mississippi, where they went door-to-door to encourage voter registration and organize Freedom Schools for black children (see Document 17). The Klan murdered three participants (two white northerners, Andrew Goodman and Michael Schwerner, and their black coworker, James Chaney), and President Lyndon Johnson ordered the Federal Bureau of Investigation (FBI) and the U.S. Navy to search for their bodies. At a high cost, SNCC's strategy worked: The national press covered it all, fascinated by white students risking their lives in the Deep South. When the MFDP challenged the all-white regular delegation at the Democratic National Convention in Atlantic City that summer, Johnson imposed a compromise in which the Freedom Democrats got two at-large delegates instead of replacing the white "regulars." LBJ was unwilling to break completely with segregationists in his party, though his victory over ultraconservative Republican Barry Goldwater in the fall was all but certain. The MFDP and SNCC refused to accept this compromise and returned home even more disillusioned with white liberalism. Later that year, in December, Martin Luther King Jr. was awarded the Nobel Peace Prize.

The last great confrontation of the civil rights movement came in Selma, Alabama, in early 1965. At the climax of a bitter voter registration campaign by SNCC and SCLC, on March 7 John Lewis led a march out of town toward Montgomery, the state capital. As the protesters crossed a bridge, mounted state police charged, beating and gassing hundreds. The assault, later known as Bloody Sunday, was covered live by the national television networks. Yet again, vicious white violence led to national outrage that forced the president to act. On March 15, Johnson addressed a special joint session of Congress, demanding a comprehensive Voting Rights Act (see Document 19). Congress passed the Voting Rights Act in August 1965. With federal registrars in place, millions of southern African Americans registered to vote. By 1968, for the first time, the majority of black Americans voted. A century after the Civil War, African Americans had finally secured a national guarantee of full citizenship.

Other movements were active during 1960 to 1965, but they all remained small. Most derived their energy from the civil rights struggle. The most dynamic involved white college students in the North.

The first widespread northern campus protests took place in the spring of 1960, when thousands of college students demonstrated outside local branches of nationwide chain stores such as Woolworth's, where the southern sit-ins were concentrated. Over the next two years, support for civil rights aided the growth of a new national group, Students for a Democratic Society (SDS), based at the University of Michigan in Ann Arbor. SDS built its reputation through solidarity with SNCC, and in June 1962 it convened a conference of forty campus leaders. They produced the Port Huron Statement (see Document 11), which emphasized a "participatory democracy"—the right of everyone to share actively in making decisions about how a society should be run. In 1963, SDS launched the Economic Research and Action Project (ERAP), a community-organizing drive modeled on SNCC and aimed at the interracial poor living in northern cities. ERAP did not become a mass movement, but hundreds of new organizers were recruited, and SDS rapidly became the most dynamic group among white students.

Campus rebellions began, however, not with SDS but with the Free Speech Movement at the University of California at Berkeley in 1964. Berkeley had developed a core of experienced activists through years of protests against the House Committee on Un-American Activities (HUAC), in support of revolutionary Cuba, and through a wide variety of other causes. Student radicals around the country looked to the San

Francisco Bay Area, especially the Berkeley campus, as an oasis of freethinkers (see Document 9). Alarmed after civil disobedience campaigns by students against racially discriminatory local businesses, the university administration announced a new policy banning any on-campus political activity not related to the campus itself. On October 1, 1964, a student was arrested for handing out leaflets in support of SNCC. Someone shouted that students should sit down around the police car holding him, and several thousand students blockaded the cruiser for thirty-two hours, using its roof as a platform to deliver speeches. Angry at what they saw as an infringement of their basic democratic rights, students launched the Free Speech Movement (FSM), which included a broad spectrum of students, from supporters of Republican presidential candidate Barry Goldwater to young Communist Party members, but was led by radicals. Over the next several months, the FSM became a mass movement involving thousands. Buildings were occupied, hundreds were arrested, and national attention was focused on Berkeley. Eventually, the FSM won the faculty's support and forced the administration to rescind all restrictions on political action. This victory signaled the emergence of a national student movement, as students everywhere emulated Berkeley's militancy and the demand to be treated like adults rather than children under an indirect form of parental control. FSM leader Mario Savio's charge that the university was complicit in social injustice had other implications: Were students being trained to be cogs in the machine of corporate capitalism, and if so, what could they do about it? (See Document 18.)

Meanwhile, the peace movement expanded. The most dramatic development was Women's Strike for Peace, a network of self-declared housewives that called a nationwide strike in November 1961. Evoking their authority as mothers, fifty thousand women took to the streets pushing baby carriages and demanding an end to the nuclear threat. Another new disarmament organization, the Student Peace Union, led a rally of five thousand students at the White House in 1962. Chastened by the Cuban missile crisis of late 1962, when the United States was on the brink of nuclear war, President Kennedy concluded the first major arms-control agreement of the cold war era, the Limited Test Ban Treaty with the Soviet Union. Signed in 1963, this treaty ended nuclear explosions in the earth's atmosphere. Many in the peace movement justifiably took credit for making the public aware of the dangers of such testing, thus prompting Kennedy to act.

The most radical challenge to the cold war orthodoxy, though short-lived, was support for Fidel Castro's revolution in Cuba. By early

1960, most Americans agreed that Castro was a menace, as he nationalized U.S.-owned businesses and proclaimed a foreign policy independent of U.S. interests (Castro did not declare himself a Communist until 1962). American journalists who knew Castro and liberals who admired Cuba's efforts to help the poor organized a public relations campaign in support of Cuba's self-determination. The Fair Play for Cuba Committee (FPCC) began with a *New York Times* advertisement in April 1960 and grew into a national organization with dozens of chapters. Castro was especially popular among students and African Americans, who admired his efforts to eradicate segregation. When Castro visited New York to speak at the United Nations in September 1960, he stayed in a Harlem hotel to the delight of the African American population there. That Christmas, FPCC sent hundreds of students to Cuba, just before President Eisenhower imposed a travel ban. When Cuban exiles led by the Central Intelligence Agency (CIA) invaded Cuba at the Bay of Pigs on April 17, 1961, the Fair Play for Cuba Committee led a wave of protests against the invasion (see Document 8). By the end of 1961, however, the group had fallen apart under pressure from congressional committees and the FBI.

In the early 1960s, women's supporting roles as wives, mothers, secretaries, and girlfriends were taken for granted. Even so, many women were quietly rebelling against rigid gender roles, and feminist activism existed within some mainstream groups. The American Association of University Women, for example, had campaigned for decades against discrimination in higher education, which kept all but a few women out of professional schools. A distinctive brand of labor feminism had been nurtured by the increase in women's union membership from 800,000 to 3 million between 1940 and 1952. Female labor leaders worked tirelessly for equal pay legislation, finally convincing Congress to pass an equal pay for equal work bill in 1962. Although the National Woman's Party, a survivor of the suffrage movement, lobbied for an equal rights amendment to the U.S. Constitution, trade union women opposed such an amendment, claiming that it would strike down a host of protective legislation.

Women active in the Old Left had inherited a critique of "male supremacy" from the Communist Party. One of these women, Betty Friedan, worked as a freelance writer during the 1950s. Like many radicals during the Red Scare, she denied her left-wing past. But in 1963, Friedan published *The Feminine Mystique,* an instant bestseller demanding solutions to "the problem that has no name": women's oppression, what radicals later labeled patriarchy (see Document 12).

Focusing on the frustrations of women who were limited to roles as housewives, Friedan articulated a new brand of rights-oriented feminism just as the civil rights movement peaked.

By the early 1960s, feminism was surfacing in liberal political circles, although most activist women avoided the word. Professional and labor union women active in the Democratic Party contributed significantly to John Kennedy's presidential campaign in 1960. His response in 1961 was the President's Commission on the Status of Women, groundbreaking in its recognition that the status of women *was* a problem. This highly respectable body performed a quietly subversive role by allowing hundreds of women to meet, analyze, and issue detailed reports on discrimination. It also created fifty state-level Commissions on the Status of Women, which in turn led to the formation of more grassroots networks. In 1964, as the Civil Rights Act moved toward passage, feminists, led by Michigan Congresswoman Martha Griffiths, pushed for the bill to include the elimination of gender-based discrimination in employment. In the end, they achieved their goal as a result of an amendment by a segregationist Virginia congressman who tried to derail the bill by adding the word *sex* to it (see Document 16). The bill passed as amended, and Title VII of the Civil Rights Act became the catalyst for sweeping challenges to discrimination against women in employment, higher education, and sports. But first feminists faced the challenge of getting the new Equal Employment Opportunity Commission (EEOC) to consider sex discrimination as more than a joke.

Least visible in these years was the tiny movement to secure civil rights for homosexuals, a group completely without legal protections, subject to losing their jobs if exposed, and widely regarded as deviants. The early 1960s saw small breakthroughs for gays. Although homosexual rights organizations had existed in Europe since the late nineteenth century, they were unknown in the United States until the Mattachine Society was founded in 1950. It remained obscure, as did the lesbian Daughters of Bilitis (DOB), which was founded in San Francisco in 1955. Neither protested constant police raids on gay bars, which had spread nationwide after young gays and lesbians had banded together in the port cities and military camps of World War II. Instead, the few local Mattachine and DOB chapters were social organizations promoting respectability. In the early 1960s, however, dissidents such as Franklin Kameny of the Washington, D.C., Mattachine Society argued for a more aggressive strategy of legal action and protest based on the civil rights movement. Kameny and others also denounced the idea that homosexuality was a sickness, insisting that different sexual preferences were equally legitimate. In San Francisco, gay men and bar owners fed up with police harassment created the Society for Individual Rights, a political infrastructure that proved it was possible to mobilize gays as voters. The first organized demonstrations for gay rights took place in 1965, sponsored by the East Coast Homophile Organizations, a new regional coalition.

By 1965, a New Left had emerged, led by the civil rights movement. As the Vietnam War escalated in the mid-1960s, cold war liberalism fractured, and multiple radical movements came forward. Instead of consensus, America began to polarize.

THE COLD WAR CONSENSUS CRACKS, 1965–1968

The three years from 1965 to 1968 saw the rise of the anti–Vietnam War, Black Power, and women's liberation movements. These movements helped destroy the liberal consensus, as Vietnam turned into a quagmire, African Americans in desolate inner cities rebelled, and women examined and contested their oppression. The period is framed by Democratic president Lyndon Johnson sending U.S. ground troops to Vietnam in March 1965 and Republican Richard Nixon winning the presidency in November 1968. In between, cold war liberalism collapsed from its own contradictions. Even without Vietnam, Johnson's enormous coalition could not have survived: He had won reelection in 1964 with 61 percent of the vote, carrying forty-four states. Resting on both southern white and northern black voters, the Democratic Party was inherently unstable. Vietnam tore at it from all directions. The war alienated working-class families who saw their sons drafted while college students got automatic draft deferments. African Americans were disproportionately represented in frontline units. The elite universities, from Berkeley to Harvard, became hotbeds of dissent. Some young whites dropped out of mainstream society, joining the "hippie" counterculture based on communal living, drugs, and sexual experimentation. Ultimately, a section of the military itself turned against the war.

The war radicalized America in two ways. First, it dragged on with no end in sight. Johnson poured in troops, reaching 543,000 by 1968. U.S. commanders constantly claimed that they saw "light at the end of the tunnel," while hundreds of U.S. soldiers died every week. Second, it was a brutal war. Americans saw television reports of enormous bombing raids that lit up the Vietnamese jungle with napalm. U.S. generals reported killing hundreds of thousands of Communist guerrillas, but viewers of the evening news saw only terrified women and children and burning villages. Many Americans began questioning the morality of the world's strongest military exerting its full force on a small peasant country.

The war's escalation, rising American casualties, and the sense that the U.S. government was committing a great wrong and lying about what was taking place in Vietnam propelled the civil rights, antinuclear, and student movements to coalesce into a larger antiwar movement. It began with a march organized by SDS in April 1965, just as the troop buildup began. Twenty thousand people attended, making it the largest peace protest since the beginning of the cold war (see Document 20). That spring, "teach-ins" at campuses across America drew tens of thousands into all-night classes, lectures, debates, and workshops on the war. By late 1965, the first national antiwar coalition brought together a wide range of protesters, from Communists to pacifists to SNCC and SDS organizers.

The antiwar movement grew steadily in 1965–67. The most rapid growth came on college campuses, as SDS mushroomed from five thousand members in 1965 to tens of thousands by 1968, part of a large-scale radicalization of young people against "the Establishment." New groups and new types of protest kept emerging. A decentralized network of draft resisters, called the Resistance, motivated thousands of men to burn their draft cards and either accept jail sentences or flee to Canada (see Document 26). Sixty thousand fled the country by war's end. In 1966, Martin Luther King Jr. helped form Clergy and Laity Concerned about Vietnam, and in the spring of 1967 he took up the cause of moral opposition to the war (see Document 27). Crowds flocked to antiwar rallies, which on April 15, 1967, attracted 200,000 people in New York and another 50,000 in San Francisco.

Yet politicians in both parties remained strongly supportive of the war through 1967. The antiwar movement was still an unpopular minority, and only a handful of those in Congress were willing to challenge the president. Organizers searched for ways to escalate their protests. In October 1967, 100,000 people marched on the Pentagon and nonviolently barricaded the seat of U.S. military power. Weeks later, Senator Eugene McCarthy of Minnesota announced that he would challenge Johnson in the Democratic primaries as an antiwar candidate. Thousands of activists joined his campaign. On January 31, 1968, South Vietnam's Communist-led National Liberation

Front, popularly known as the Vietcong, proved its strength with the devastating Tet Offensive, battling U.S. forces in every city in that country. Weeks later, McCarthy almost beat Johnson in the bellwether New Hampshire primary, an almost unprecedented repudiation of a sitting president. In March, Democratic senator Robert F. Kennedy announced his own antiwar candidacy. On March 31, Johnson withdrew from the race and initiated negotiations with the Vietnamese Communists.

The second blow to the liberal consensus was the black freedom movement's demand for not just rights but power—Black Power. At the time, the Black Power movement seemed like a shocking departure from the interracial protests of the civil rights movement. The linkage of "black" and "power" deeply unsettled white people, who found it hard to accept that African Americans would demand the power whites already had. When the slogan emerged in 1966, Black Power was associated with a group of charismatic young men, including SNCC chairman Stokely Carmichael, Huey P. Newton of the Black Panther Party, and the martyred Malcolm X. Journalists focused on phrases such as "by any means necessary" and "picking up the gun" and on spectacular images of fists punching the air, Afro hairdos, and young black men holding shotguns. Since then, scholars have explained Black Power as an expression of the rage felt by civil rights activists over their betrayal by white liberals. The catalog of betrayals included the federal government's refusal to protect civil rights workers from violence, the failure to act against de facto segregation in the North, attempts by white liberals to control the civil rights movement, and the humiliation of the Mississippi Freedom Democrats at the Democratic National Convention in 1964. These explanations are only partially correct. Important civil rights organizations did break their alliances with white liberals. In 1965–66, for example, SNCC and CORE, formerly interracial, decided that they would be exclusively black and vowed to redirect their attention to the urban North. But the Black Power movement had deeper roots, tied to the long-brewing crisis of America's inner cities, the so-called ghettos to which southern blacks had moved since World War I.

In the 1950s, high-paying, unionized factory jobs were the primary road to economic security for black men. But during that decade, corporations started moving factories to non-union states and overseas, and a long process of deindustrialization began. In addition, white-run municipal governments embarked on urban renewal programs, called "Negro removal" by African Americans whose homes and neighborhoods were demolished. White resistance to "open housing" was well organized, and a black family moving into a white block in Philadelphia, Detroit, or any of the new suburbs typically faced stone-throwing mobs and firebombs. Thus northern African Americans were increasingly trapped in decaying, jobless urban neighborhoods. At the same time, overwhelmingly white police forces were aggressively hostile toward blacks.

These conditions led to dozens of urban rebellions, inaccurately labeled "riots," that exemplified Black Power's explosive possibilities. From Birmingham, Alabama, in 1963; to Harlem in 1964; the Watts neighborhood of Los Angeles in 1965; and Newark, New Jersey, and Detroit in 1967, they demonstrated that America's cities were ungovernable under the old rules of white control. Each summer, the uprisings became bigger and more destructive. Most began with crowds angered by white police arresting black men and escalated into sweeping assaults on white businesses and the entire apparatus of law and order. The culmination came in April 1968, when a white supremacist assassinated Martin Luther King Jr. in Memphis. In response, 109 cities erupted in violence.

The ideology of Black Power drew on many influences, from anti-imperialist struggles in the third world to the Nation of Islam's call for self-reliance. Since the early 1960s, dozens of local organizations had formed in northern cities such as Detroit, Chicago, Oakland, and Cleveland. These groups advocated pride in being black and self-determination rather than assimilation into white middle-class society. Malcolm X spoke for all of them, paving the way for Black Power. When Stokely Carmichael made the first widely publicized demand for Black Power during a June 1966 march in Mississippi, he immediately found a national audience among African Americans, although liberals of both races reacted with outrage. Then, in October 1966, the Black Panther Party for Self-Defense (BPP) was founded in Oakland by two community college students, Huey P. Newton and Bobby Seale (see Document 22). The Panthers were truly new—the first armed revolutionary organization of African Americans in U.S. history. At first, they patrolled Oakland with legally registered weapons and law books in hand, monitoring police behavior ("policing the police"). In May 1967, they became world famous when Seale led an armed delegation into California's state capitol building and held a press conference denouncing a law aimed at stripping them of their guns. The BPP's paramilitary structure either thrilled or horrified people. For many African Americans, it was liberating to see young African Americans arm themselves. Yet the BPP was never typical of the Black Power movement, which focused primarily on community building and local electoral power, and the Panthers' embrace of violence alienated potential allies and brought down intensive government repression.

Unlike the antiwar movement, with its single goal of ending the war, Black Power advocates had many objectives. Simply put, they wanted to change all of the conditions of life in Black America. The question was, how? Many activists, such as Stokely Carmichael, urged organizing a voting bloc to elect African American leaders and take over city governments, as European immigrant groups had done throughout U.S. history (see Document 24). By contrast, the Panthers called not just for self-defense but also for "revolutionary nationalism," waging armed struggle against the police and ultimately the federal government. Other Black Power activists, such as Maulana Karenga, defined themselves as "cultural nationalists" and focused on changing black consciousness and developing an African-centered worldview rather than on revolution (see Document 25). Some even advocated getting white corporations and the government to fund a new black capitalism.

From 1966 on, these strategies competed with one another. National Black Power Conferences were held in 1967, 1968, and 1969, but no consensus emerged. The white media, the FBI, and local white politicians focused on "black militants," especially the BPP, as an immediate threat. In December 1967, Newton went to jail after a shootout in Oakland in which a police officer died. For the next three years, the Panthers carried out a massive "Free Huey" campaign. Seeking a longer-term impact, the larger Black Power movement pursued grassroots empowerment and cultural development through hundreds of local community centers, theater companies, schools, cooperatives, and bookstores. Everywhere, activists noted that despite millions of African American voters, only a tiny handful of black officials were elected nationwide. The demand for representation became a central focus of the movement.

The period 1965–68 also saw the beginnings of a feminist upsurge. From 1964 to 1966, women in unions and professional organizations called on the new EEOC to enforce the ban on sex discrimination in Title VII of the Civil Rights Act. In August 1966, however, it became apparent that women needed their own organization to pressure the government to enforce the law. At the annual meeting of the state Commissions on the Status of Women, government officials squashed a resolution calling on the EEOC to take action. In response, Betty

Friedan convened a caucus of a few veterans of the women's rights movement. The result was the formation of the National Organization for Women (NOW). Led by New Yorkers such as Friedan and by mid-western union activists, NOW was conceived as a feminist equivalent of the NAACP (see Document 23). Open to men as well as women, it supported women's advancement and combated discrimination through protests and litigation. Then and later, many labeled NOW's brand of women's rights as "liberal feminism," but the results of its activism were ultimately radical. Meanwhile, a "radical feminist" critique came to the fore within SNCC and SDS.

Younger women did much of the practical work in the student-based left. Even in these organizations, women were still expected to abide by the gender roles of the 1950s: They were helpmates, girl-friends, and assistants. They took notes, made coffee, and got out mailings, while men dominated leadership bodies, led debates, and wrote articles. At a SNCC retreat in late 1964, a few women who were experienced movement veterans circulated an anonymous "Position Paper (Women in the Movement)," comparing the treatment of African Americans as second-class citizens with the treatment of women in SNCC. In response, Stokely Carmichael commented, "The only position for women in SNCC is prone," meaning ready for sex. The following year, these women sent a memo to women nationwide (see Document 21), prompting a debate in SDS. As SDS grew in 1966–67, women began to assert themselves in the organization, holding their own workshops and refusing to be silenced by men's insults. At SDS's national conference in 1967, a women's liberation workshop forced the organization to go on the record against male supremacy.

In late 1967, the first radical feminist "small group" was founded in Chicago (it was called simply the "Westside group"). This and other small groups were local, volunteer-based, informal organizations. None tried to reproduce themselves nationally, or even outside their own cities. Their refusal to formalize a hierarchical leadership structure with bylaws and elected officers was one of the truly radical things about radical feminism. Throughout 1968, local women's liberation groups sprang up nationwide. Although some were very influential, such as New York Radical Women (NYRW; see Document 29), which organized the first national protest by radical feminists at the 1968 Miss America pageant in Atlantic City, New Jersey (see Document 30), each had its own distinctive ideology and ways of operating. What they had in common was anger over the sexism of many male activists and a commitment to serious intellectual exploration of how women were oppressed—in classrooms, workplaces, the bedroom, and even their own self-image. Ultimately, the practice of consciousness-raising, a structured sharing of experience and pain, became the main organizational tool of the new feminism (see Document 40). Hundreds of thousands of women participated in consciousness-raising groups, learning to analyze patriarchy as a system of oppression, not just the individual problem of individual women. As 1968 ended, feminism was ready to emerge as a mass movement. Radical women had left behind groups such as SDS, and sexual politics—the politics of abortion, rape, and lesbianism—was on the horizon.

The year 1968 had a larger significance in world history. For a few months, massive demonstrations, strikes, and disruptions throughout the world seemed to portend a global revolution. In France, striking students and workers paralyzed the country. In Mexico City, government forces massacred hundreds of students during demonstrations. In Czechoslovakia, a reform Communist government sought "socialism with a human face," until it was squashed by Soviet tanks. In the United States, the year began with the Tet Offensive. At the end of March, President Johnson announced that he would not seek reelection. On April 5, Martin Luther King Jr. was assassinated, and cities across the country started to burn. Later that month, SDS activists and African American students occupied buildings at Columbia University to protest the university's racist practices toward the adjoining Harlem neighborhood. Although the protesters were violently expelled by police, with hundreds of injuries and arrests, the strike stimulated many more student occupations, as college campuses became battlegrounds.

In May, a new wave of antiwar activism emerged among radical Catholics. The Catholic Church relied on tens of thousands of parishes and schools staffed by devoted priests and nuns. When a few of them began protesting the war, it sent shock waves through Catholic America, a pillar of anticommunism. This insurgency drew on the Catholic Worker movement, a pacifist counterculture within the church led by Dorothy Day. On May 9, Daniel and Philip Berrigan, working-class priests from Minnesota, led a raid on a draft board in Catonsville, Maryland, pouring their own blood over thousands of files and then burning them before submitting to arrest (see Document 28). Over the next four years, hundreds of devout Catholics joined in acts of resistance to the war.

As spring moved into summer, the violence only worsened. The nation was still reeling from Martin Luther King Jr.'s assassination when

Robert Kennedy was assassinated the night he won the pivotal California primary in June. In August, thousands of antiwar activists, including the anarchist Youth International Party, or Yippies, led by Abbie Hoffman and Jerry Rubin, converged on Chicago to protest at the Democratic National Convention. By that time, Democratic Party chiefs, including Chicago mayor Richard Daley, had guaranteed the nomination to pro-war vice president Hubert Humphrey. During the convention, Daley unleashed his police force on protesters. Police beat hundreds of protesters and gassed thousands more over several nights—all of which was broadcast live on national television. According to polls, a majority of the public supported Daley's actions.

As the Democratic Party and cold war liberalism fractured, Richard Nixon easily secured the Republican nomination, claiming that he sought "peace with honor" and "law and order." In November, he narrowly defeated Humphrey, while a renegade Democrat, former Alabama governor George Wallace, won five southern states as a third-party conservative. Between them, Nixon and Wallace received 57 percent of the vote, solidifying a national constituency opposed to everything the New Left stood for. By January 1, 1969, it was clear that some kind of tide had turned. The left was no longer allied with liberals in power, the government was now unequivocally the enemy, and the country had entered a period of profound division. As if to signal this polarization, just before Christmas 1968 Mike Klonsky, the national secretary of SDS, called for a "revolutionary youth movement" that would leave college campuses and join with working-class people to challenge capitalism and imperialism directly (see Document 32). Given SDS's visibility after 1965, as well as moves by many youth and student organizations toward a consciously revolutionary position and the development of a "new communist movement," his proposal had a considerable impact.

HIGH TIDE AND EBB TIDE, 1969–1975

The New Left's high tide corresponded with Nixon's presidency. He was its worst adversary, and activists of all stripes were united by their opposition to him and to the war he insisted on prolonging. For a few years, roughly 1969 to 1971, a host of new movements surged forward, inspired by the third world. It seemed as if the United States might be on the verge of revolution. All the "invisible" people—African Americans, Chicanos, Native Americans, Puerto Ricans, Asian

Americans, gay liberationists, and radical and lesbian feminists— demanded power.

Nixon was a sophisticated politician, not a true conservative. In Vietnam, he focused on avoiding defeat by a policy called "Vietnamization," withdrawing U.S. troops while increasing bombing. Simultaneously, he exploited the growing conservative backlash, deploying his demagogic vice president, Spiro Agnew, to attack leading Democrats as "radical liberals." His administration prosecuted New Left and antiwar leaders across the board on charges such as crossing state lines with the intention of inciting a riot, while the FBI stepped up its covert disruptions. Nixon's attempts to repress all opposition polarized the country, and as a result the antiwar movement became a mainstream force. To students, ministers, pacifists, and professors were added many members of Congress, business and union leaders, college presidents, and bishops. In October 1969, a new coalition called for a nationwide day of reflection to register one's opposition to the war in school, at work, or on the streets. Millions participated in this Moratorium, including twenty-four senators and many religious leaders. The following month, at least 500,000 people gathered in Washington, D.C., for the largest antiwar rally to date.

Protest and violence flared again in April 1970, when Nixon tried to regain the military initiative by illegally invading neutral Cambodia. Three hundred colleges officially closed during a nationwide strike against the invasion involving 1.5 million students. On May 4, at Kent State in Ohio, National Guardsmen fired into a crowd of students, killing four (see Document 41). Two days later, Mississippi State Police shot up a dormitory at all-black Jackson State, killing two more students. The spring of 1970 seemed a desperate time, as Nixon called students "bums" and congratulated New York construction workers who attacked protesters with steel pipes. Steadily, the peace bloc in Congress expanded, as antiwar activists were elected to the House and senior senators offered bills calling for immediate withdrawal of U.S. troops from Vietnam. A striking sign of the breadth of activism was the organization Vietnam Veterans Against the War (VVAW), led by Navy Lieutenant John Kerry, later a Massachusetts senator and presidential candidate. In April 1971, during the last big mobilization, eight hundred VVAW members threw away their medals on the steps of the U.S. Capitol (see Document 43). In early May, more than twelve thousand members of the Mayday Tribe were arrested when they tried to shut down Washington, D.C., completely. This was the largest civil disobedience protest in U.S. history.

After the fiasco of 1968, the Democratic Party's presidential nomination process was opened up in 1972, so that voters in primaries rather than party bosses could choose the majority of delegates and thus the nominee. The 1972 presidential campaign brought much of the antiwar movement into the party, backing the Senate's antiwar leader, George McGovern of South Dakota, who won the Democratic nomination. Nixon trounced McGovern in the general election, as Republicans charged that Democrats stood for "acid, abortion, and amnesty." ("Amnesty" was a reference to pardons for draft resisters, whom conservatives considered deserters.) To guarantee his victory, Nixon finally concluded peace negotiations with North Vietnam. In January 1973, the United States withdrew its last combat troops, while the fighting between North and South Vietnam continued unabated. For Americans, at least, the war was over, a defeat in every sense—politically, militarily, and morally. In April 1975, the South Vietnamese regime collapsed, and Vietnam was finally unified under the Communists.

For the Black Power movement, the Nixon years marked a sharp break from decades of liberalism. The president was openly hostile to African American rights and pursued a "southern strategy" to appeal to white southerners. As "white flight" from urban areas accelerated, repression by police and government agencies intensified. Most black activists pursued pragmatic strategies to acquire a share of power and protect themselves. For decades, civil rights and Black Power leaders had advocated that African Americans assert themselves as a voting bloc to control city services and jobs. After 1968, southern African Americans elected hundreds of local officials in counties with black majorities. In the North, even the most radical Black Power activists focused on mobilizing voters. Victories in mayoral elections highlighted this trend. For the first time in American history, significant numbers of whites were directly governed by African Americans. Cleveland, Los Angeles, Atlanta, and Detroit, as well as Newark, New Jersey, and Gary, Indiana, elected black mayors between 1967 and 1974. The number of African Americans in Congress increased from six in 1964 to thirteen in 1970. Black representatives formed the Congressional Black Caucus (CBC) in 1971 (see Document 44), shocking white liberals used to treating African American politicians as loyal junior partners. The CBC rapidly asserted its influence with the Democratic leadership and sought to represent Black America in negotiations with the White House and the rest of the federal government.

While black politicians claimed electoral victories, other black activists were hounded, jailed, and killed in significant numbers. There was a clear intent by the federal government, allied with local authorities, to crush the militant wing of the Black Power movement, and this plan was largely successful. Several dozen Black Panthers died in police raids on their offices or homes (see Document 39). In Chicago, Panther leaders Fred Hampton and Mark Clark were shot to pieces while sleeping. Others went into exile. Internal schisms turned violent, in part because FBI infiltrators encouraged purges and revenge killings. In 1971, BPP chairman Bobby Seale was tried for the murder of an informant in New Haven, Connecticut, where even the president of Yale University said Seale could not get a fair trial. He was acquitted, but many other Panthers were convicted and received long sentences. In August 1970, Huey Newton was released from jail. Earlier, he had declared that the Panthers should "serve the people," and the BPP had initiated popular free-breakfast programs and other community services. In 1972, however, Newton shut down the national organization and ordered the Panthers' hard-core members back to Oakland, where he constructed an old-style political machine with criminal sidelines.

Just as Black Power became institutionalized in local and national government, it also put down roots on college campuses through hundreds of black studies programs. Parallel to the political movement was a renaissance of poetry, fiction, dance, theater, painting, and filmmaking dubbed the Black Arts Movement. The culmination of the Black Power movement was the National Black Political Assembly, held in Gary, Indiana, in March 1972. Attended by eight thousand delegates and observers, it was chaired by Detroit congressman Charles Diggs Jr. and the renowned poet and playwright Amiri Baraka, who had helped elect Newark, New Jersey's first black mayor in 1970. But the unity of the Gary convention was short-lived. Some cultural nationalists, such as Baraka, joined the New Communist Movement (see pages 34–35), while most activists moved into the Democratic Party, academia, and government jobs. As the 1970s progressed, the Black Power movement faded away but a significant degree of black power was institutionalized.

In the late 1960s, many other movements among people of color arose, emulating the Black Power movement's emphasis on self-determination, pride, and reclaiming one's identity. Native American, Chicano, Asian American, and African American students organized Third World Liberation Fronts (TWLFs) at San Francisco State University and Berkeley in late 1968 and early 1969. The TWLFs catalyzed the emergence of a third world identity inside the United States that was linked to the liberation movements in Africa, Asia, and Latin America.

They led strikes on these two campuses to demand the creation of ethnic studies programs, which they hoped would overcome the institutional racism and powerlessness each group faced (see Document 31). In conjunction with other protests, confrontations, and occupations, these strikes signaled the emergence of new movements, each with its own geographic center and specific demands.

In the 1950s, Native Americans in desperately poor rural reservations and urban ghettos faced cultural extinction through a government policy of forced assimilation. In response, hundreds of distinct tribes created a pan-Indian identity, called the Red Power movement, during the 1960s. They demanded that old treaties be honored, that Native American culture be respected, and that Indians regain control over their lives from the government's paternalistic Bureau of Indian Affairs (BIA).

Red Power had its roots in the 1950s, when so-called "traditionals" fought to retain treaty rights on reservations. In 1961, a new college-educated generation founded the National Indian Youth Council (NIYC) to challenge the older leadership of Indian rights groups. The NIYC called for pride in Indian identity and a protest strategy, something new among Native Americans. These trends culminated in the November 1969 takeover of Alcatraz Island, the site of a former federal prison in San Francisco Bay, by a coalition called Indians of All Tribes (see Document 37). They took advantage of a treaty granting Indians the right to occupy unused federal land. Dreams of converting Alcatraz into a university and spiritual center collapsed, but the occupation galvanized a new national consciousness among Native Americans. Over the next few years, seizures of unused federal land multiplied.

The American Indian Movement (AIM) came to prominence as a group prepared to physically confront abusive white authorities and assert Indian pride. Tough, articulate AIM leaders, such as Dennis Banks and Russell Means, organized a series of armed showdowns across the Great Plains, gaining enormous media attention. In 1972, AIM and other groups organized caravans from around the country that followed the "Trail of Broken Treaties" to Washington, D.C., where they briefly occupied the BIA building. As with the Black Panthers, however, the possibility of violence overshadowed the community organizing and legal strategies pursued by the larger Native American movement. The climax came in February 1973, when AIM came to the aid of Sioux traditionals under attack by a conservative tribal government on South Dakota's Pine Ridge Reservation. AIM led an armed takeover of Wounded Knee, the site of the last massacre of Native Americans by U.S. troops, in 1890. They held the village for six weeks, defying the FBI, U.S. Army units, and local vigilantes. These confrontations produced few concrete results, but they raised the stakes. If the "first Americans" took up arms, was the United States itself in jeopardy? AIM soon collapsed under the weight of hundreds of prosecutions and FBI repression, but the Indian renaissance continued in subsequent decades. Activists took over tribal governments, dozens of Native American colleges opened, and old treaties were successfully litigated, gaining major economic benefits for tribes. Rather than dying out, the self-identified Native American population grew rapidly.

Like Native Americans, Chicanos (Mexican Americans) were a conquered people, living in the southwestern states that had been seized from Mexico in 1848. Since then, their land had been stolen, and they had been politically neutralized and often segregated. Returning World War II veterans and first-generation college students stimulated new political involvement in the 1940s and 1950s. In the 1960s, a Chicano movement coalesced. Key to this resurgence was the United Farm Workers (UFW), a union led by the charismatic, devoutly Catholic pacifist César Chávez. Beginning in California's Central Valley in 1965, Chávez led a series of strikes and boycotts among migrant lettuce and grape pickers, who were among the poorest workers in the country. Engaging in grueling hunger strikes and practicing nonviolence, Chávez was widely compared to Martin Luther King Jr. The UFW garnered great support among whites, including Catholic liberals such as Senator Robert Kennedy. In the 1970s, it recruited hundreds of young white organizers to implement a nationwide grape boycott and won the first-ever union contracts for agricultural laborers.

The farm workers symbolized the Chicanos' plight, but they were only one part of the Chicano movement. In 1968, high school students organized mass walkouts (called blowouts) to protest racism in Los Angeles high schools. Early the following year, they joined with college students to form the Movimiento Estudiantil Chicano de Aztlán (MEChA), or the Chicano Student Movement of Aztlán. (Aztlán was an Indian name for the Southwest region; see Document 36.) MEChA and other Chicano groups were cultural nationalists, emphasizing their Indian heritage and the importance of language and tradition, and repudiating assimilation into "Anglo" (white) culture. These youths took the word *chicano,* used as a pejorative label for working-class Mexicans of Indian background, to claim a positive new consciousness. The Chicano movement also had an electoral wing, which mobilized local majorities. The Raza Unida (United Race) party briefly enjoyed success in Texas in 1970–71. Within a few years, however, Chicano activists gravitated back to the Democratic Party, which for decades had sought Mexican Americans' votes but had excluded them from representation. Political institutions such as the Southwest Voter Registration Education Project, founded in 1974, greatly expanded the number of Mexican American voters, as well as the number of Latino (Chicano and other Hispanic) elected officials. The Hispanic Caucus also emerged in Congress.

Puerto Ricans were relatively new immigrants who had settled in large numbers in New York City and the Northeast since World War II. Their radicalism focused on independence for Puerto Rico, which had been a U.S. colony since 1898, and the racism they faced in the States. The most famous Puerto Rican radical organization was New York's Young Lords Party (YLP), led by working-class college students and modeled on the Black Panthers. Defying the police, staging street protests, and organizing community services in East Harlem in 1969–71, the Lords became heroes to many, despite their advocacy of revolution (see Document 34). The YLP did not last long, but in the early 1970s the Puerto Rican Socialist Party (PSP), which called for the island's independence from the United States, attracted thousands of supporters in the U.S. and even organized a massive Madison Square Garden rally in October 1974. Despite these efforts, Puerto Rican radicalism waned in the mid-1970s, while many YLP and PSP veterans went on to prominence in journalism, academia, and politics. Puerto Ricans also emerged as a significant constituency, electing members of Congress and establishing a network of legal, social, and community institutions.

Asian Americans, too, developed a collective identity in these years. The major groups—Japanese, Chinese, Korean, and Filipino Americans—had little in common in Asia, where they spoke different languages and sometimes made war on one another. In the United States, however, racial stereotyping and deeply rooted nativist hostility toward all Asian immigrants pushed these peoples together. This trend accelerated after 1965, when Congress overturned the 1927 ban on Asian immigration, and the Asian American population grew rapidly. Young Asian Americans rebelled against both cultural assimilation and the conservative businessmen who controlled the Japantowns and Chinatowns in East and West Coast cities. The Communist revolutions in Vietnam and China had a special appeal to many of these activists as assertions of national independence. By becoming a recognized ethnic group, Asian Americans were able to develop academic programs and a host of community organizations focused on immigrants, while also asserting themselves as voters.

For feminists, 1969 to 1973 was a period of extraordinary success. The mass media discovered women's liberation in 1969. A flood of sensationalized stories created new celebrities out of movement intellectuals. Consciousness-raising spread nationwide as the shared experience of all feminists, whatever their differences. The following year saw two crucial watersheds, both revolving around the rapidly expanding NOW. In May 1970, NOW convened its Second Congress to Unite Women. A group of lesbians wearing T-shirts emblazoned with the phrase LAVENDER MENACE rushed the stage and took over the proceedings, forcing participants to listen to their complaints of how lesbians had been silenced and scorned by the mainstream movement. Through confrontations like this, radical lesbians compelled the feminist movement to confront the issue of women who love women. Despite attempts to purge gay women by NOW president Betty Friedan, who feared that a strong lesbian presence would drive straight women away and leave the feminists open to accusations of being "man haters," the movement moved rapidly to recognize sexual freedom of choice as a basic right. Lesbianism was out of the closet for good.

Later that year, NOW organized the first nationwide feminist protest since World War I. On August 26, tens of thousands of women nationwide marched in the Women's Strike for Equality, demanding abortion rights, an end to discrimination in employment and education, and free day care so that women could work to support themselves. This action signaled a political maturation. During the 1970s, NOW grew exponentially into a major national organization, with hundreds of chapters, state organizations, and a professional staff. It also became a powerful political lobby, helping to convince Congress to pass the Equal Rights Amendment (ERA) in 1971 (House) and 1972 (Senate). In 1972, Congress also passed Title IX of the Education Amendments, requiring equal funding and opportunities for women at all educational institutions receiving federal support. These efforts were facilitated by feminists such as Bella Abzug (see Document 42) who were elected to Congress.

Many new organizations also were founded, such as the National Women's Political Caucus in 1971 and coalitions to support ratification of the ERA by the states, which drew in traditional women's groups. In 1970, one such organization, the Women's Equity Action League, filed a class action suit against every university in the United States. The suit demonstrated sweeping discrimination in academic hiring and led to systematic affirmative action efforts in later decades. Other caucuses and organizations sprang up in academic disciplines, male-dominated trade unions, among athletes, and elsewhere. Increasingly, their attention turned to issues of sexual violence—the rape and wife abuse that police routinely ignored. Take Back the Night marches began, and hundreds of women's shelters opened, leading to fundamental shifts in how the government and legal authorities operated. Police forces stopped treating wife abuse as a strictly domestic matter. Laws barring accused rapists from citing a rape victim's sexual history in court were passed. A culminating victory was the U.S. Supreme Court's *Roe v. Wade* decision in 1973. This decision legalized abortion, a revolutionary change giving women control over their bodies.

By the mid-1970s, feminism, as "the simple proposition that women are fully human," had pervaded popular culture, facilitated by intense media coverage and its own *Ms.* magazine, founded in 1972. Top-rated television shows such as *The Mary Tyler Moore Show* made heroines out of independent, explicitly feminist young women. Most striking, perhaps, was the development of a radical consciousness among women about their bodies and the medical profession. The enduring success of the grassroots guide *Our Bodies, Ourselves* demonstrates this shift in awareness. Developed by a local Boston collective in 1970, it has sold millions of copies since its publication (see Document 45). In all these ways, rather than merging into the mainstream and losing its radical edge, feminism took over the mainstream, angering both men and women who valued traditional gender roles. Throughout this period, however, women's liberation was limited by its concentration on the concerns of white middle-class women, and black and Chicana feminist groups developed on their own. Early on, the Third World Women's Alliance (TWWA) issued a strong critique of the racial myopia of many white feminists (see Document 33). Others criticized the tendency to assume that all women had a college education and the lack of attention to the struggles of working-class women for basic economic security rather than opportunities for professional advancement. The Coalition of Labor Union Women was founded in 1974 with the purpose of reorienting feminism toward economic and class issues.

Why was feminism so successful in these years, even though it broke all the rules for effective movements? It had few well-funded national organizations, other than NOW. There were deep divisions between different groups: liberals versus radicals versus socialists versus lesbians. Instead of a single, sharp focus, the movement constantly took on new issues, such as combating domestic violence, supporting women's businesses, and generating a feminist theology. Ultimately, all these apparent weaknesses proved to be strengths. Like Black Power, feminism succeeded because it was as much a cultural revolution, a new way of understanding the world, as an organized movement. Anywhere, on any day, an American woman could decide that she was a feminist and act on that conviction: by applying for a "man's job," by speaking up instead of remaining silent, by changing how she behaved around men. Women's liberation was fundamentally a movement of self-liberation, through millions of individual decisions spurred by friendships and support groups, books and magazines. Although the ERA failed to be ratified by a sufficient number of states, the movement's success was extraordinary.

Feminism had a long history, but no more than a handful of homophile activists in the Mattachine Society and other tiny groups had imagined a movement for homosexual freedom and power. When gay liberation rose up spectacularly after the Stonewall riot of 1969, most of the New Left was ambivalent or hostile. The Stonewall Inn was a tavern frequented by street people and drag queens in New York's Greenwich Village. Police raided it late on June 27, 1969. Gays gathered as struggling patrons were led out in handcuffs. The crowd swelled to two thousand and started throwing objects, driving the frightened police into the building. For several nights, angry gay men fought running battles with police as word spread nationally. Inspired by this uprising, New Yorkers formed the Gay Liberation Front (GLF) in July. Bursting with rhetoric that linked freedom from sexual oppression to the war in Vietnam and repression of the Black Panthers, GLF members went on the road to form branches in other cities. They mocked the older homophile activists and promoted a homosexual revolution. Instead of seeking privacy, they encouraged "coming out"—declaring one's sexuality to friends, family, and coworkers and projecting pride instead of shame (see Document 35). Gays operating within other radical organizations came out, and gay contingents appeared at all the major antiwar events.

Like other New Left movements, gay liberation benefited from sensationalized media coverage. Yet, as with women's liberation, the new excitement obscured existing gay activism that had been steadily expanding since 1965. In 1966, fifteen local groups founded the North American Conference of Homophile Organizations. By early 1969, it had grown to encompass fifty organizations, reaching into cities such as Cincinnati and Phoenix. In 1968 in Los Angeles, *The Advocate,* the first national gay magazine, began publication. At the same time, the Metropolitan Community Church, a new Christian denomination for homosexuals, was founded in Los Angeles. By 2000, the church had three hundred congregations throughout the United States. Meanwhile, in New York and San Francisco, the Mattachine Society and similar groups won significant political victories. In 1966, for instance, the New York city school system stopped automatically firing teachers exposed as being gay. These early advances set the stage for the GLF and other gay rights organizations.

In December 1969, some members of the GLF left to form the Gay Activists Alliance (GAA), a model for gay rights organizations in the 1970s. Unlike the GLF, the GAA was consciously a single-issue organization, avoiding other radical causes (see Document 38). It perfected the technique of the "zap," breaking into public events to embarrass liberal New York City mayor John Lindsay and other officials with shouted demands for equal rights. The GLF was intensely suspicious of hierarchy, written rules, and structures. In contrast, the GAA had a complex committee structure and a formal decision-making process based on voting rather than consensus. In 1971, the GAA bought an old firehouse in lower Manhattan and began holding profitable weekly dances. These events became the center of gay men's socializing in New York.

Around the country, openly gay neighborhoods spread, especially in San Francisco and New York, with gay-run businesses, restaurants, street festivals, and political clubs. Activists emulated the GAA, pressuring liberal politicians to endorse gay rights. In 1972, gays in San Francisco's Alice B. Toklas Democratic Club led a nationwide effort to back George McGovern's presidential campaign in return for his endorsement of homosexual rights. Activists also made a top priority of forcing the American Psychiatric Association to eliminate its official classification of homosexuality as a mental illness. After years of protest, the association voted in December 1973 to remove homosexuality from its list of recognized disorders, a step of enormous consequence because it eliminated one basis for official discrimination against gay people. As public acceptance increased, wealthy gay men formed the National Gay Task Force in 1973, an explicitly moderate group akin to NOW or the NAACP. Gays also began to win political office. Elaine Noble, an open lesbian, was elected to the Massachusetts legislature in 1974, and in 1977 San Francisco's leading gay activist, Harvey Milk, was elected to the Board of Supervisors. The following year, he and Mayor George Moscone were assassinated by a conservative former supervisor.

Although the gay liberation movement flourished during these years, it also faced deep divisions. Most evidently, gay culture was dominated by gay men and their quest for sexual exploration and liberation. While gay women fought against homophobia in the women's movement, they also battled against male supremacy in the gay movement. At marches commemorating the Stonewall riot each summer, some lesbians took offense at drag queens parading a version of femininity that many women had repudiated. Many lesbians grew tired of men, whatever their sexual orientation, and withdrew into a women's culture of entirely female lives and associations. In that sense, the gay and lesbian movement was always an uneasy coalition. By the mid-1970s, it was recognized as a political interest group but still loathed by many heterosexual Americans. Little has changed since then. Gays are a growing political force that includes members of Congress, but many major political and religious figures still view homosexuality as a disease or mental illness. Only in 2003 did the U.S. Supreme Court finally strike down state laws mandating criminal penalties for the types of sexual acts engaged in by gays.

As we have seen, the late 1960s and early 1970s saw the rise of many movements that remained separate from one another. During these years, there was also a failed attempt to build a unified revolutionary movement for an assault on capitalism, imperialism, and the U.S. government itself. For a few years, thousands of young activists from all the different movements imagined that they could turn society upside down. The best-known example of this move toward revolutionary politics is the breakup of SDS, the largest student radical group. By 1969, its leaders all defined themselves as revolutionaries and argued about the proper strategy to overthrow capitalism. The debates were fierce: Should students leave their campuses and take factory jobs? Or should they create an urban guerrilla movement? SDS broke apart at a tumultuous national convention in June 1969. One faction created Weatherman, an underground organization dedicated to "bringing the war home." Weatherman never achieved much—it planted a few bombs, and some of its members died trying to build bombs—but the idea of white college students living on the run and taking up revolutionary terrorism obsessed the public. Although the vast majority of former SDS members did not join Weatherman, the mass media made the few hundred who did notorious.

Most of the new revolutionaries did not agree with Weatherman's strategy of armed struggle by a few urban guerrillas. Instead, they decided that the times called for a disciplined revolutionary party to organize America's working class. They looked to Mao Zedong's

People's Republic of China, Cuba, and Vietnam for inspiration; the Soviet Union was derided as corrupt. The so-called New Communist Movement created a host of small, centralized organizations, each with a few hundred members, its own newspaper, and plans for infiltrating their activists into steel and auto factories and coal mines. After a few years of furious effort, all of these "pre-party formations" declined in the late 1970s. For the most committed radicals, this failure was massive. There was no frontal assault on capitalism. To their chagrin, instead of working-class revolution, most of the New Left found a home in the emerging left wing of the Democratic Party.

CONCLUSION: THE MOVEMENTS GO THEIR OWN WAY

The early 1970s were a chaotic time. Exploiting a conservative backlash among whites, President Nixon swept to reelection in November 1972. Within two years, he was forced from office because of the criminal conspiracies called Watergate. In those years, most of the New Left's movements put down permanent roots, but their revolutionary dreams faded. As each movement went its own way, the idea of a New Left united by a common radical commitment faded, too. Activists reacted differently. To some, this was a period of collapse, symbolized by the disappearance of SDS, SNCC, and other groups; government repression; and the dispersion of radical energies. Others remembered the victories, whether ending the war or winning abortion rights, and saw the New Left's end as the beginning of long-term gains in power. There was one definite closure in these years: the U.S. defeat in Vietnam. The antiwar movement was the common ground shared by all activists, from Betty Friedan to Bobby Seale. With the U.S. withdrawal from Vietnam in 1973 and Nixon's resignation in 1974, that common cause was gone. Nixon's successor, Gerald Ford, asserted in September 1974 that "our long national nightmare is over." He was referring not just to Watergate but also to the war in Vietnam and the confrontations at home. His expression of relief spoke to the desire for civic peace and the diminished possibility of a radical upsurge.

The New Left realigned U.S. politics in two ways. First, by 1974 segments of each of the radical movements had been incorporated into the Democratic Party via George McGovern's 1972 presidential campaign, the Congressional Black Caucus, campaigns by movement leaders for elective office, and the formation of new organizations to lobby Congress. Cold war liberalism was dead. In its place was a radical liberalism led by feminists, gays, antiwar protesters, and people of color, who found a new home in the party of FDR and LBJ. Over subsequent decades, the Democrats have attempted to balance the demands of their grassroots activists with the moderate politics associated with Presidents Jimmy Carter and Bill Clinton. Second, while the Democratic Party incorporated the left, conservatives took over the Republican Party. A New Right, born in the 1960s, grew rapidly in the 1970s, using widespread resentments of New Left radicalism as a road to power. New Right leaders built alliances between traditional economic conservatives and new social movements opposed to abortion, gay rights, gun control, pornography, and busing to achieve school integration. White men, especially southerners and blue-collar workers, defected to the Republicans in large numbers. For the next thirty years, two opposing coalitions—the New Left movements around the fractured Democratic Party and the New Right dominating the Republican Party—battled for advantage.

What were the long-term results of the New Left's many movements? Were they successful? Given the ascendance of conservative politics, epitomized by Presidents Ronald Reagan and George W. Bush, some scholars assert that the United States has turned to the right, repudiating the movements of the New Left. But if they are correct, we should see reversals of the radical changes in American politics, law, and culture that occurred between 1954 (the year of *Brown v. Board of Education*) and 1973 (the year of *Roe v. Wade*). There has been no such reversal. The "rights revolution" has not been overturned. Rather, it has put down permanent roots and in many cases has extended the claims of radical democracy even further.

First, the Civil Rights Act of 1964 and the Voting Rights Act of 1965 together marked a revolutionary change in extending full citizenship to all Americans. That revolution remains firmly in place. Equal treatment before the law and in all public activities, from business to education, is enforceable and enforced. There is no longer any "right to discriminate" (as Ronald Reagan once called it), whether in selling a house or admitting a person to college. Nor is any state or locality permitted to limit the right to vote, the exception being state laws disenfranchising people convicted of felonies, which have been used to disenfranchise many poor people of color. Because we take these rights for granted, it is easy to forget that they were won through decades of sacrifice by ordinary people. John Kennedy, Lyndon Johnson, and the U.S. Congress did not initiate these great reforms. Instead, they supported them late and under enormous pressure from a powerful movement led by African Americans.

Second, once the civil rights movement broke through the walls of legal discrimination and disenfranchisement, other marginalized constituencies streamed into that opening. One after another, they carved out a political place and won new rights. Following the example of African Americans, they demanded to be represented by their own. Until the 1970s, elective offices from the county courthouse to the U.S. Senate were reserved for the white male minority. Now we are becoming accustomed to seeing women, gays, and black, brown, red, and yellow faces in positions of power. Some would say that changing the complexion or gender of power accomplishes little, that having a conservative female officeholder or a gay or black Republican makes no difference in the process. If this were the case, why did it take so long to accomplish? Why are most Americans still impressed that Colin Powell could be secretary of state, and why do most find it hard to imagine a woman becoming president? Concretely, political representation of these constituencies helps guarantee that newly won rights will not be taken away. There are few, if any, black, Latino, Native American, or Asian American officeholders who would vote to limit enforcement of civil rights laws, or few women who would vote to overturn bans on gender discrimination and sexual harassment.

Changes in politics and law are only some of the revolutionary changes the New Left made in American life. Its influence is even more deeply embedded in our culture—how we behave, what we assume, the language we use. A half-century ago, the normative American citizen was a heterosexual white man; women were appendages, mothers, wives, or daughters whose identities were bound up with men. The position of people of color was worse. Their grasp on citizenship was tenuous, subject to the whims of white policemen, officials, and employers. Women of color were doubly oppressed (or triply, if one remembers that most lived in poverty). Homosexuals did not exist as a social category outside the criminal code and textbooks on mental illness. Look around a city, college campus, school, or workplace now, and see how much has changed. People of color and women routinely occupy positions of authority—though white men still dominate. Most girls in America are told by their mothers and teachers (and even their fathers) to safeguard their independence as equals of men. Certainly, racism remains pervasive, reflected in the grossly disproportionate rates of unemployment and imprisonment suffered by African Americans and Latinos. But outright white supremacy, historically ingrained in American culture, is no longer legally or socially acceptable. An overt racist runs the serious risk of losing his or her job, as judges, college presidents, school principals, and military commanders are required by law to punish displays of racism. Gay people are least protected from discrimination but are pushing hard against the barriers that define them as less than equal, whether to secure their right to the protections afforded by marriage, their right to serve their country, or their right to equal treatment on the job.

Finally, the movements of the New Left contributed to a radical extension of democracy, by breaking down the Red Scare's limits on freedom of expression. From the late 1940s into the 1960s, anyone challenging U.S. foreign policy risked being called a "Communist sympathizer" and losing his or her job. Wars, interventions, a peacetime draft, a massive military buildup, and CIA covert operations throughout the third world took place with no meaningful opposition. The New Left broke the cold war consensus through unyielding opposition to the war in Vietnam. It guaranteed that since then, there has been continuous debate, and often sustained protest, against military interventionism, the arms race, and U.S. support of foreign dictatorships. In the Nuclear Freeze campaign, and the movements in solidarity with revolutions in Central America and opposing apartheid in South Africa of the 1980s, as well as in the protests against the war in Iraq in recent years, a healthy space for dissent has remained open. We now accept protest, even during wartime, as thoroughly American.

To understand the radicalism of the New Left requires an understanding of the profound limits on democracy that existed for most of America's history. It took not one but many movements, over several decades, to cut through the web of legal, cultural, and institutional constraints that made the majority of Americans "second-class" in their own country because of their color, ethnicity, gender, sexual orientation, or beliefs. The battle between the New Right, born in the 1960s, and the descendants of the New Left may continue for a long time to come. The possibility of a radical democracy based on the absolute civil equality of all persons remains highly contentious. It violates many people's belief in a natural order, where men and women play distinct roles and the United States is defined as a country of white Christian heterosexuals in which all others are guests—or second-class citizens. The New Left's movements made the premise of the Declaration of Independence, that all human beings are created equal, a tangible reality for the first time. The question now becomes, as Martin Luther King Jr. asked in 1967, where do we go from here?

PART TWO

The Documents

1

MATTACHINE SOCIETY

Statement of Purpose

1951

Gay liberation is often described as the New Left's last major movement, starting in 1969. Gay politics actually began much earlier, however, at the Red Scare's height, as a forerunner of the New Left and a legacy of the Old Left. In 1950, Harry Hay and several other former Communists in Los Angeles created what they called a "homophile" organization (a word implying acceptance of homosexuality), the Mattachine Society. Its Statement of Purpose anticipated both the New Left's focus on personal dignity and empowerment and the gay movement's eventual turn toward politics. Hay left the Mattachine Society in 1953, after which the organization became much more cautious, functioning more like a private support group than an activist organization. Its main public activity was to invite experts in law and psychology to give lectures, in hopes that would encourage greater tolerance of homosexuals.

Reprinted in Mark Blasius and Shane Phelan, eds., *We Are Everywhere: A Historical Sourcebook of Gay and Lesbian Politics* (New York: Routledge, 1997), 283.

1. *To Unify*—While there are undoubtedly individual homosexuals who number many of their own people among their friends, thousands of homosexuals live out their lives bewildered, unhappy, alone—isolated from their own kind and unable to adjust to the dominant culture. Even those who may have many homosexual friends are still cut off from the deep satisfactions man's gregarious nature can achieve *only* when he is consciously part of a larger unified whole. A major purpose of the Mattachine Society is to provide a consensus of principle around which all of our people can rally and from which they can derive a feeling of "belonging."

2. *To Educate*—The total of information available on the subject of homosexuality is woefully meagre and utterly inconclusive. The Society organizes all available material, and conducts extensive researches itself—psychological, physiological, anthropological, and sociological—for the purpose of informing all interested homosexuals, and for the purpose of informing and enlightening the public at large.

The Mattachine Society holds it possible and desirable that a highly ethical homosexual culture emerge, as a consequence of its work, paralleling the emerging cultures of our fellow minorities ... the Negro, Mexican, and Jewish Peoples. The Society believes homosexuals can lead well-adjusted, wholesome, and socially productive lives once ignorance, and prejudice, against them is successfully combatted, and once homosexuals themselves feel they have a dignified and useful role to play in society. The Society, to these ends, is in the process of developing a homosexual ethic ... disciplined, moral, and socially responsible.

3. *To Lead*—It is not sufficient for an oppressed minority such as the homosexuals merely to be conscious of belonging to a minority collective when, as is the situation at the present time, that collective is neither socially organic nor objective in its directions and activities—although this minimum is in fact a great step forward. It is necessary that the more far-reaching and socially conscious homosexuals provide leadership to the whole mass of social deviants if the first two missions (the unification and the education of the homosexual minority) are to be accomplished. Further, once unification and education have progressed, it becomes imperative (to consolidate these gains) for the Corporation to push forward into the realm of political action to erase from our law books the discriminatory and oppressive legislation presently directed against the homosexual minority.

The Society, founded upon the highest ethical and social principles, serves as an example for homosexuals to follow, and provides a dignified standard upon which the rest of society may base a more intelligent and accurate picture of the nature of homosexuality than currently obtains in the public mind. The Society provides the instrument necessary to work with like-minded and socially valuable organizations, and supplies the means for the assistance of our people who are victimized daily as a result of our oppression. Only a Society, providing an enlightened leadership, can rouse the homosexuals ... one of the largest minorities in America today ... to take the actions necessary to elevate themselves from the social ostracism an unsympathetic culture has perpetrated upon them.

2

COLEMAN YOUNG

Testimony Before the House Committee on Un-American Activities

February 28, 1952

Public hearings by legislative bodies such as the House Committee on Un-American Activities (known as HUAC, pronounced "hew-ack") were the best-known feature of the Red Scare. Thousands of leftists were grilled about their beliefs and activities and pressured to "name names"—that is, to inform on others. Uncooperative witnesses usually lost their jobs and were blacklisted, the main punishment for radicals during the Red Scare. In 1952, HUAC had a difficult time with a Detroit trade unionist, Coleman Young. He was executive secretary of the National Negro Labor Council, which advocated for African American rights in the workplace and unions and had many Communist members. Young's combative appearance boosted his reputation among blacks in Detroit, and phonograph records of his testimony launched his political career as a Democrat. He was elected mayor of Detroit in 1973, a position he held for twenty years. The African American community was the one part of U.S.

House Committee on Un-American Activities, *Communism in the Detroit Area—Part I* (Washington, D.C.: Government Printing Office, 1952), 2878–93.

society where the Red Scare was not completely effective, because the Communists had been the strongest supporters of complete racial equality.

... *Mr. Tavenner:*[1] Will you state your full name, please, Mr. Young?

Mr. Young: Coleman A. Young.

Mr. Tavenner: When and where were you born?

Mr. Young: May 24, 1918, Tuscaloosa, Ala.

Mr. Tavenner: Will you tell the committee, please, briefly, what your education training has been?

Mr. Young: I am a high school graduate.

Mr. Tavenner: Do you now reside in Detroit?

Mr. Young: I do.

Mr. Tavenner: How long have you lived in Detroit?

Mr. Young: Approximately 30 years.

Mr. Tavenner: Will you give the committee, please, a general background of your employment record, say, over the past 10 years?

Mr. Young: Well, I came out of high school and I went to work at Ford Motor Co. — that was in 1937 — for about a year and a half. I subsequently worked in a dry-cleaning plant; I worked for the United States Veterans' Administration, at the hospital here; I worked for the post office before I went into the Army.[2] I was discharged from the post office for attempting to organize a union. I went into the Army about a month later. After coming out, I worked for the post office about 2 months. I quit the post office because they refused to give me a leave of absence so that I might work for the union organization, the International Union of United Public Workers; director of program for the Wayne County CIO [Congress of Industrial Organizations]; State director for the Progressive Party[3] of Michigan; presently, national executive secretary of the National Negro Labor Council. ...

Mr. Tavenner: Mr. Young, I want to state to you in advance of questioning you, that the investigators of the committee have not produced or presented any evidence of Communist Party membership

---

[1] Frank Tavenner, a Virginian, was counsel to HUAC.

[2] Young was an officer in the famous Tuskegee Airmen, the all-black fighter squadron, and aggressively challenged segregation in the military.

[3] The Progressive Party was a short-lived, left-wing party that split from the Democrats after World War II. In 1948, it ran former vice president Henry Wallace for president. He received 2 percent of the vote and was attacked for accepting the support of the Communist Party.

on your part. The purpose in asking you to come here is to inquire into some of the—into the activities of some of the organizations with which you have been connected, to see to what extent, if any, the committee should be interested in them from the standpoint of those manifesting communism. Now, you mentioned—

Mr. Young: Mr. Tavenner, I would like to say this: First of all, I have understood, from official pronouncements of this committee, and yourself, that this is a forum; you call it the highest forum in the country, being that of the Congress of the United States. I have been subpoenaed here. I didn't come by my own prerogative.

Mr. Tavenner: I understand.

Mr. Young: I can only state that in being interviewed and being asked questions, that I hope that I will be allowed to react fully to those questions, and not be expected to react only in such a manner that this committee may desire me. In other words, I might have answers you might not like. You called me here to testify; I am prepared to testify, but, I would like to know from you if I shall be allowed to respond to your questions fully and in my own way.

Mr. Tavenner: I have no objection to your answers, if they are responsive to the questions.

Mr. Young: I will respond.

Mr. Tavenner: But I desire to ask you the question which I have asked other witnesses: Are you now a member of the Communist Party?

Mr. Young: I refuse to answer that question, relying upon my rights under the fifth amendment, and, in light of the fact that an answer to such a question, before such a committee, would be, in my opinion, a violation of my rights under the first amendment, which provides for freedom of speech, sanctity and privacy of political beliefs and associates, and, further, since I have no purpose of being here as a stool pigeon, I am not prepared to give any information on any of my associates or political thoughts.

Mr. Tavenner: Have you been a member of the Communist Party?

Mr. Young: For the same reason, I refuse to answer that question.

Mr. Tavenner: You told us you were the executive secretary of the National Negro Congress—

Mr. Young: That word is "Negro," not "Niggra."

Mr. Tavenner: I said, "Negro." I think you are mistaken.

Mr. Young: I hope I am. Speak more clearly.

Mr. Wood:[4] I will appreciate it if you will not argue with counsel.

---

[4]Representative John S. Wood, Democrat of Georgia, was chairman of HUAC.

Mr. Young: It isn't my purpose to argue. As a Negro, I resent the slur-
ring of the name of my race.
Mr. Wood: You are here for the purpose of answering questions.
Mr. Young: In some sections of the country they slur—
Mr. Tavenner: I am sorry. I did not mean to slur it.

3

JO ANN ROBINSON

Letter to Mayor W. A. Gayle

May 21, 1954

*African American activists had been organizing in Montgomery, Ala-
bama, since World War II. Among the leaders was Jo Ann Robinson, an
English professor at a local college and president of the Women's Political
Council (WPC), a group allied with the Montgomery branch of the
NAACP. For more than a year before Rosa Parks was arrested for refusing
to give up her seat on a bus to a white man (December 1, 1955), Robinson had pressured the city to modify its humiliating policies regarding
bus segregation. The WPC helped initiate the Montgomery bus boycott
(1955–57), mimeographing 40,000 leaflets at Robinson's college on the
night of Parks's arrest.*

Herriet St.
Montgomery, Ala.
May 21, 1954

Honorable Mayor W. A. Gayle
City Hall
Montgomery, Alabama

Dear Sir:
The Woman's Political Council is very grateful to you and the City
Commissioners for the hearing you allowed our representatives dur-

Reprinted in Jo Ann Gibson Robinson, *The Montgomery Bus Boycott and the Women Who
Started It: The Memoir of Jo Ann Gibson Robinson,* ed. David J. Garrow (Knoxville: University of Tennessee Press, 1987), viii.

ing the month of March, 1954, when the "city-bus-fare-increase case" was being reviewed. There were several things the Council asked for:

1. A city law that would make it possible for Negroes to sit from back toward front, and whites from front toward back until all the seats are taken;
2. That Negroes not be asked or forced to pay fare at front and go to the rear of the bus to enter;
3. That busses stop at every corner in residential sections occupied by Negroes as they do in communities where whites reside.

We are happy to report that busses have begun stopping at more corners now in some sections where Negroes live than previously. However, the same practices in seating and boarding the bus continue.

Mayor Gayle, three-fourths of the riders of these public conveyances are Negroes. If Negroes did not patronize them, they could not possibly operate.

More and more of our people are already arranging with neighbors and friends to ride to keep from being insulted and humiliated by bus drivers.

There has been talk from twenty-five or more local organizations of planning a city-wide boycott of busses. We, sir, do not feel that forceful measures are necessary in bargaining for a convenience which is right for all bus passengers. We, the Council, believe that when this matter has been put before you and the Commissioners, that agreeable terms can be met in a quiet and unostensible manner to the satisfaction of all concerned.

Many of our Southern cities in neighboring states have practiced the policies we seek without incident whatsoever. Atlanta, Macon and Savannah in Georgia have done this for years. Even Mobile, in our own state, does this and all the passengers are satisfied.

Please consider this plea, and if possible, act favorably upon it, for even now plans are being made to ride less, or not at all, on our busses. We do not want this.

Respectfully yours,
The Women's Political Council

Jo Ann Robinson, President

4

ROSA PARKS

The Montgomery Bus Boycott:
Talk at the Highlander Folk School

March 1956

Rosa Parks is famous as the middle-aged African American seamstress who refused to give up her seat on a bus to a white man and was arrested for disobeying local segregation laws. But she was also a long-time civil rights activist—secretary of the Montgomery, Alabama, chapter of the NAACP and a participant in workshops at the Highlander Folk School. Since the 1930s, Highlander, located in the Tennessee mountains, had been an outpost of the Old Left in the South, a place where blacks and whites, Christians and Communists, studied methods of nonviolent protest known collectively as passive resistance. Parks's arrest on December 1, 1955, sparked a long-planned bus boycott by the African Americans of Montgomery. In March 1956, in the midst of the boycott, Parks returned to Highlander. Her talk highlighted the importance of using disciplined nonviolence to attract media attention and thus arouse the consciences of people around the world. The strategies pioneered by the civil rights movement in the Deep South were subsequently used by all the movements of the New Left.

Rosa Parks: Montgomery today is nothing at all like it was as you knew it last year. It's just a different place altogether since we demonstrated, which marked the time of my arrest on the city line bus for not moving out of the seat I had already occupied. For a white person to take the seat I would have had to stand. It was not at all pre-arranged. It just happened that the driver made a demand and I just didn't feel like obeying his demand. He called a policeman and I was arrested and placed in jail, later released on a $100 bond and brought to trial on December 5th. This was the first date

---

Reprinted in Joanne Grant, ed., *Black Protest: History, Documents, and Analyses, 1619 to the Present* (New York: Fawcett, 1968), 277–79.

that the Negroes of Montgomery set to not ride the bus and from December to this date they are still staying off the bus in large numbers, almost 100%. Once in a while you may see one or two but very seldom do you see any riding the city line buses. It attracted much attention all over the nation and world wide, you may say. There was attention even as far away as London. We had a correspondent at one of our meetings. There was a correspondent from even as far away as Tokyo, Japan. People all over the country have called in to see what's going on, what's being done and what is the reaction to it.

Myles Horton:[1] What you did was a very little thing just to sit there, you know, to touch off such a fire. Why did you do it; what moved you not to move? . . .

Rosa Parks: Well, in the first place, I had been working all day on the job. I was quite tired after spending a full day working. I handle and work on clothing that white people wear. That didn't come in my mind but this is what I wanted to know; when and how would we ever determine our rights as human beings? The section of the bus where I was sitting was what we called the colored section, especially in this neighborhood because the bus was filled more than two-thirds with Negro passengers and a number of them were standing. And just as soon as enough white passengers got on the bus to take what we consider their seats and then a few over, that meant that we would have to move back for them even though there was no room to move back. It was an imposition as far as I was concerned.

Myles Horton: Well, had you ever moved before?

Rosa Parks: I hadn't for quite a long while. It has happened in the past and I did obey somewhat reluctantly. The times that I had to move back I think a colored man gave me his seat. Just having paid for a seat and riding for only a couple of blocks and then having to stand, was too much. These other persons had got on the bus after I did—it meant that I didn't have a right to do anything but get on the bus, give them my fare and then be pushed wherever they wanted me. . . .

Beulah Johnson:[2] You ask what has happened to Rosa. I think I can tell you what happened to her. It is the same thing that happened to

---

[1] Myles Horton was the longtime director of the Highlander Folk School and one of the South's most respected white radicals from the 1930s to the 1980s.

[2] Beulah Johnson was another activist working on the Montgomery bus boycott.

me. . . . I was tired of insults. You know that the law is on your side and you get tired of being run over. You say, "Well, let's fight it out—if it means going to jail then go to jail." That's just the whole attitude—when you get tired then you get tired of people asking you to get up and move. I'm just pretty certain that that's just one of those days that happened to Rosa. There comes a time in your life when you just decide that you don't give a rap. Many of us have reached that point. I don't live in Montgomery but I'm in Montgomery every week and I know the situation. Now that's what happened to Rosa here. You ask the question why people fell in line.

We have had NAACP meetings and we've had the things we discussed when we were here last summer. We have been very much concerned with getting people registered in the state of Alabama. We've been talking about those things and we've been reviewing what has happened all around as far as the court decisions go.

Myles Horton: Well, that answers a lot of questions in my mind—but it still doesn't explain why it took the passive resistance form that it did.

Rosa Parks: I think I can account for that because in the organization the ministers came together and took the lead and made the announcements from their pulpits and we also had these spiritual mass meetings twice weekly.

Beulah Johnson: Well, I tell you I think you are going to have to keep in mind that for the last five years we have been calling on ministers throughout the United States and we have been letting them know that it is strictly a job that ministers should undertake. There has been beautiful support from the ministers—they are really coming out and working. I think they are simply doing what should have been done a long time ago. . . .

5

LIBERATION

Tract for the Times: Editorial

March 1956

In 1956, pacifists founded Liberation, *a key magazine of the New Left over the next decade. Many of its editors and writers had met during World War II in the Civilian Public Service camps, where conscientious objectors performed manual labor.* Liberation's *founders, including A. J. Muste, Dave Dellinger, and Bayard Rustin, played major roles in the development of the New Left. Muste and Dellinger helped create and lead the major anti–Vietnam War coalitions. Rustin worked closely with Martin Luther King Jr., coordinating the August 1963 March on Washington. This editorial appeared in the magazine's first issue.*

The decline of independent radicalism and the gradual falling into silence of prophetic and rebellious voices is an ominous feature of the mid-twentieth century. Anxiety and apprehension have invaded the air we breathe. Advances in science and technology, which should have been our greatest triumphs, leave us stunned and uncertain as to whether human life and history have meaning.

Power is everywhere openly or secretly idolized. The threat of atomic or biological war, perhaps even the extinction of mankind, hangs over the earth. Hopes and ideals have become propaganda devices. But those who should furnish vision and direction are silent or echoing old ideas in which they scarcely believe themselves.

This failure of a new radicalism to emerge is an indication, it seems to us, that the stock of fundamental ideas on which the radical thinking of recent times has been predicated is badly in need of thorough reappraisal. Much of its inspiration appears to be used up. Old labels—principally in the Marxist and liberal traditions—simply do not apply anymore, and the phrases which fifty years ago were guideposts to significant action have largely become empty patter and jargon.

Reprinted in Paul Goodman, ed., *Seeds of Liberation* (New York: George Braziller, 1964), 3–11.

The changes of recent years—represented by atomic power and by the beginnings of the Second Industrial Revolution and also by the rise of totalitarianism—have filled many thoughtful persons with the strong suspicion that the problems of today must be attacked on a much deeper level than traditional Marxists, Communists and various kinds of Socialists and Anarchists have realized. Proposals and calls to action couched in the old terms fail any longer to inspire much hope or genuine humane enthusiasm, because large numbers of people are aware, or dimly sense, that they do not touch the roots of the trouble.

There is no point, for example, in reshuffling power, because the same old abuses still persist under new masters. The vast energy devoted to reconstructing government is wasted if in a short time the new structure becomes as impervious to fundamental human decency and ethics as the old one. There is no doubt that there are forms of property relationships which are oppressive and destructive of true community, but if these are altered and the average individual finds his life as dull and empty as ever and the enslavement of his hours just as great, little or nothing has been achieved. . . .

The Politics of the Future

One of the symptoms of our time is that many people are fed up with "politics"—by which they mean the whole machinery associated with political life. To become significant, politics must discover its ethical foundations and dynamic.

The politics of the future requires a creative synthesis of the individual ethical insights of the great religious leaders and the collective social concern of the great revolutionists.

It follows that we do not conceive the problem of revolution or the building of a better society as one of accumulating power, whether by legislative or other methods, to "capture the State," and then, presumably, to transform society and human beings as well. The national, sovereign, militarized and bureaucratic State and a bureaucratic collectivist economy are themselves evils to be avoided or abolished. Seizure of the war-making and repressive machinery of the State cannot be a step toward transforming society into a free and humanly satisfying pattern. It is the transformation of society by human decision and action that we seek. This is a more complex and human process in which power as ordinarily conceived plays a minor part. Political action in this context is, therefore, broadly conceived. . . .

Similarly, we reject the faith in technology, industrialization and centralization *per se,* characteristic of both the contemporary capitalist and Communist regimes. Our emphasis is rather on possibilities for decentralization, on direct participation of all workers or citizens in determining the conditions of life and work, and on the use of technology for human ends, rather than the subjection of man to the demands of technology. . . .

The problem of war is one of special gravity for us, as for all our fellow men. It may be argued that for personal ethics there is no distinction between a war in which a few persons are killed at a time and one in which multitudes are wiped out. But from a sociological view, the H-bomb and what it symbolizes—possible extinction of the race itself—present mankind with a new situation. War is no longer an instrument of policy or a means to any rational end. For this reason, if for no other, a central part of any radical movement today is withdrawal of support from the military preparation and activities of *both* the dominant power blocs. Whatever differences may exist between Communist and "free world" regimes, in this decisive respect they are *equal* threats, two sides of the *same* threat to the survival of civilization. The H-bomb is not an instrument of peace in the hands of one and of war in the hands of the other. Nor is it a mere accidental excrescence in either of them but, rather, a logical outgrowth of their basic economic and social orders. . . .

Liberation will seek to inspire its readers not only to fresh thinking but to *action now*—refusal to run away or to conform; concrete resistance in the communities in which we live to all the ways in which human beings are regimented and corrupted, dehumanized and deprived of their freedom; experimentation in creative living by individuals, families, and groups; day to day support of movements to abolish colonialism and racism or for the freedom of all individuals from domination, whether military, economic, political, or cultural.

6

COMMITTEE FOR A SANE NUCLEAR POLICY

We Are Facing a Danger Unlike Any Danger That Has Ever Existed: Advertisement in the New York Times

November 15, 1957

The Committee for a Sane Nuclear Policy (SANE) was founded through a New York Times *advertisement with forty-eight sponsors, including former First Lady Eleanor Roosevelt and numerous religious and academic leaders. About 2,500 people responded to the ad, and it was reprinted in thirty-two newspapers around the country. In response to this groundswell of interest, the original sponsors created a permanent organization. Within the year, it had 130 chapters with 25,000 members. SANE steered a cautious course, enlisting scientists, movie stars, and businesspeople to rebut charges of its being pro-Communist. It made opposition to nuclear war respectable and mobilized broad support for banning nuclear tests in the earth's atmosphere. These efforts helped lead to the Limited Test Ban Treaty of 1963.*

A deep uneasiness exists inside Americans as we look out on the world.

It is not that we have suddenly become unsure of ourselves in a world in which the Soviet Union has dramatically laid claim to scientific supremacy.[1]

Nor that the same propulsion device that can send a man-made satellite into outer space can send a missile carrying a hydrogen bomb across the ocean in eighteen minutes.

Nor is the uneasiness only the result of headlines that tell of trouble between Turkey and Syria and a war that could not be limited to the Middle East.

---

[1]This reference is to the Soviet Union's launching of *Sputnik* earlier in 1957. The American public was shocked that the Soviet Union was the first to launch a vehicle into space.

Reprinted in Milton S. Katz, *Ban the Bomb: A History of SANE, the Committee for a Sane Nuclear Policy* (New York: Praeger, 1987), 27.

The uneasiness that exists inside Americans has to do with the fact that we are not living up to our moral capacity in the world.

We have been living half a life. We have been developing our appetites, but we have been starving our purposes. We have been concerned with bigger incomes, bigger television screens, and bigger cars—but not with the big ideas on which our lives and freedoms depend.

We are facing a danger unlike any danger that has ever existed. In our possession and in the possession of the Russians are more than enough nuclear explosives to put an end to the life of man on earth.

Our uneasiness is the result of the fact that our approach to the danger is unequal to the danger. Our response to the challenge of today's world seems out of joint. The slogans and arguments that belong to the world of competitive national sovereignties—a world of plot and counterplot—no longer fit the world of today or tomorrow.

Just in front of us opens a grand human adventure into outer space. But within us and all around us is the need to make this world whole before we set out for other ones. We can earn the right to explore other planets only as we make this one safe and fit for human habitation.

The sovereignty of the human community comes before all others—before the sovereignty of groups, tribes, or nations. In that community, man has natural rights. He has the right to live and to grow, to breathe unpoisoned air, to work on uncontaminated soil. He has the right to his sacred nature.

If what nations are doing has the effect of destroying these natural rights, whether by upsetting the delicate balances on which life depends, or fouling the air, or devitalizing the land or tampering with the genetic integrity of man himself, then it becomes necessary for people to restrain and tame the nations.

Indeed the test of a nation's right to survive today is measured not by the size of its bombs or the range of its missiles, but by the size and range of its concern for the human community as a whole.

There can be no true security for America unless we can exert leadership in these terms, unless we become advocates of a grand design that is directed to the large cause of human destiny. . . .

7

STUDENT NONVIOLENT COORDINATING COMMITTEE

Statement of Purpose

May 14, 1960

When the Student Nonviolent Coordinating Committee (SNCC) was founded in April 1960 as a coalition of fifty-six southern college groups, the Southern Christian Leadership Conference (SCLC) assumed that the new group would become its student auxiliary, under adult control. But SCLC's executive director, Ella Baker, was wary of what she called "leader-centered groups" and privately counseled the students to remain independent. SNCC became a self-described "beloved community," a space for young southerners, black and white, to meet as equals and practice nonviolence. This direction came from the Nashville Action Group, led by the Reverend James Lawson, a former conscientious objector, missionary in India, and field secretary for the pacifist Fellowship of Reconciliation. He drafted SNCC's Statement of Purpose, with its intensely spiritual focus derived from the Indian leader Mohandas Gandhi's politics of nonviolent direct action.

We affirm the philosophical or religious ideal of nonviolence as the foundation of our purpose, the presupposition of our faith, and the manner of our action. Nonviolence as it grows from Judaic-Christian traditions seeks a social order of justice permeated by love. Integration of human endeavor represents the crucial first step towards such a society.

Through nonviolence, courage displaces fear; love transforms hate. Acceptance dissipates prejudice; hope ends despair. Peace dominates war; faith reconciles doubt. Mutual regard cancels enmity. Justice for all overthrows injustice. The redemptive community supersedes systems of gross social immorality.

Love is the central motif of nonviolence. Love is the force by which

Reprinted in Joanne Grant, ed., *Black Protest: History, Documents, and Analyses, 1619 to the Present* (New York: Fawcett, 1968), 290.

God binds man to Himself and man to man. Such love goes to the extreme; it remains loving and forgiving even in the midst of hostility. It matches the capacity of evil to inflict suffering with an even more enduring capacity to absorb evil, all the while persisting in love.

By appealing to conscience and standing on the moral nature of human existence, nonviolence nurtures the atmosphere in which reconciliation and justice become actual possibilities.

8

FAIR PLAY FOR CUBA COMMITTEE

Cuba: A Declaration of Conscience by Afro-Americans: Advertisement in the New York Post

April 25, 1961

The Fair Play for Cuba Committee (FPCC) challenged the cold war orthodoxy that divided the world into two blocs. FPCC members agreed that Cubans had the right to choose their own government after sixty years of U.S. domination and saw Castro as a genuine revolutionary, not a Soviet puppet. When the CIA staged an invasion in April 1961, the FPCC's African American members published an advertisement in the New York Post. Signers included the eminent intellectual W. E. B. Du Bois and many key figures of the 1960s, such as the writers LeRoi Jones (later Amiri Baraka), Harold Cruse, John Henrik Clarke, and Maya Angelou, as well as Robert F. Williams, an NAACP leader in North Carolina who advocated armed self-defense and ended up as the first famous African American exile in Cuba.

Because we have known oppression, because we have suffered more than other Americans, because we are still fighting for our own liberation from tyranny, we Afro-Americans have the right and the duty to raise our voices in protest against the forces of oppression that now seek to crush a free people linked to us by bonds of blood and a common heritage.

One-third of Cuba's people are Afro-Cubans, of the same African descent as we. Many of our own forefathers passed through Cuba on their way to the slave plantations in the United States. Those who remained on the island knew the same brutality that their brothers suffered on the mainland. After emancipation, they too knew disenfranchisement, they too became second-class citizens, peons exploited on the huge U.S.-owned landholdings.

Today, thanks to a social revolution which they helped make, Afro-Cubans are first-class citizens and are taking their rightful place in the life of their country where all racial barriers crumbled in a matter of weeks following the victory of Fidel Castro.

Now our brothers are threatened again—this time by a gang of ousted white Cuban politicians who find segregated Miami more congenial than integrated Havana. We charge that this group of mercenaries who hope to turn back the clock in Cuba are armed, trained and financed by the U.S. Central Intelligence Agency. This criminal aggression against a peaceful and progressive people must not be allowed to continue. But if it does, we are determined to do all we possibly can to hinder the success of this crime.

William Worthy, foreign correspondent for the Baltimore *Afro-American,* declared recently: "If Cuba is attacked, I and others who know the facts will denounce the attack as an evil and wicked colonial war deserving of opposition and resistance by Afro-Americans." Worthy warned that, if such an attack took place: "In this country we would see civil rights setbacks from coast to coast. Our enemies would be strengthened and emboldened."

Afro-Americans won't be fooled. The enemies of the Cubans are our enemies: the Jim Crow bosses of this land where we are still denied our rights. The Cubans are our friends. The Cubans are the enemies of our enemies.

9

DALE JOHNSON

On the Ideology of the Campus Revolution

May 1961

Dale Johnson was a Stanford graduate student and executive secretary of the Palo Alto chapter of the FPCC. His account of the upsurge of Bay Area student radicalism appeared in Studies on the Left, *published by graduate students at the University of Wisconsin. He stressed the connections between activities such as the protests when HUAC came to town; the organization of a campus political party (SLATE); picketing at the Woolworth's department store to show solidarity with sit-ins at its southern branches; antinuclear protests and rallies against requiring male students to participate in the Reserve Officers' Training Corps (ROTC); and above all, the powerful influence of the Cuban Revolution in radicalizing young Americans and the sense of outrage caused by the Bay of Pigs invasion in April 1961. Like* The Port Huron Statement *(see Document 11) and the magazine* Liberation *(see Document 5), Johnson insisted that the New Left had moved beyond old ideologies, using them to create something new.*

It used to be that the wise and benevolent elder generation bemoaned the apathy and lack of direction of their offspring. They wondered at the lack of response in the college atmosphere of ideas, they were amused at the prevalence of spring water fights and panty raids, and raised their eyebrows at those who withdrew to North Beach.[1] In recent months it seems to many that a revolution has taken place on campus. Disturbed by recent student political activities, California legislators have questioned the wisdom of granting salary increases to a Berkeley faculty and administration which allowed its students to flaunt, unpunished, the "law and order" represented by the HUAC. Furthermore, U. of C. [University of California] faculty members have

---

[1]North Beach was the San Francisco neighborhood where Beat poets and artists who had dropped out of conventional society congregated in the 1950s.

Studies on the Left, 2, no. 1 (1961): 73–75.

been attacked as willing agents of the conspiracy to corrupt the pliable minds of youth.

Although many campuses are experiencing this upheaval, the center of activities seems to reside in the San Francisco Bay Area, particularly at the University of California. Space does not permit a complete analysis of the campus revolution's development but it is possible to note briefly something of the nature of the movement.

U. of C. students, by and large inactive since the 1930s, took the first step several years ago by organizing SLATE, a "liberal" campus political party. Since the inception of SLATE, which managed to stimulate, organize, and direct student protest toward the world of politics, a multitude of single-purpose groups, permanent and *ad hoc,* have sprung up. Last year the Chessman case brought on a tremendous student drive for an end to the death penalty;[2] there have been dramatic protests against compulsory ROTC; students have worked to end discrimination in housing; Woolworth's has been picketed almost daily; demonstrations against missile bases have been conducted by students with strong pacifist convictions. By far the most effective in stirring protest, however, have been the sit-ins and the demonstrations against the HUAC in San Francisco. The effective use of direct action techniques in the sit-ins and the highly dramatic nature of the anti-HUAC campaign brought nationwide attention. As a result of these instances, several thousand students of this area and throughout the country have become aware that they can express their discontent effectively by joining others of like mind on the picket line.

Since the May anti-HUAC "riots," new organizations and spontaneous protest movements have grown up; the socialist groups of the area have reported a high degree of interest in their programs.... The American Legion Convention in San Francisco last summer invited a demonstration by manhandling a few students who had the audacity to carry signs questioning the wisdom of Legion resolutions. Several hundred from this area called for civil rights and "freedom now" in front of the Democratic Convention in Los Angeles. The audience for Nixon's San Francisco speech was shocked to see students raise placards calling for "No More U-2s."[3] There was some talk, but

---

[2]Caryl Chessman was sentenced to death for a rape many believed he did not commit. Protests against his execution attracted the support of many Americans, including movie stars such as Marlon Brando. Despite this outcry, Chessman was put to death.

[3]In May 1960, it was revealed that the United States was conducting secret aerial surveillance of the Soviet Union from high-altitude U-2 spy planes when the Soviets shot down a U-2 piloted by Francis Gary Powers. This incident provoked an international crisis, since the flights were clearly illegal.

not much action, for a "Vote No For President" campaign. Finally, and I think this may prove to be the most important of all, there has been the impact of the Cuban Revolution.

To a remarkable degree there are ideological similarities between the Cuban and campus revolutions. Both Cuban and campus rebels are *strong* dissenters, firm in their convictions and willing to speak out and act militantly in spite of the mighty coercive powers of the American state. Both are pragmatic, always putting first things first, with rarely an eye to ultimate ends. In Cuba this takes the form of "the year of agrarian reform," the "year of education," the "year of industrialization." . . . Here at home the pragmatic outlook is manifested in the multitude of single-issue groups devoted simply to getting things done in the most effective manner possible. Organizations form almost overnight to work on specific questions—civil liberties, academic freedom, ROTC, the death penalty, civil rights. Both Cuban and campus revolutions are inexperienced, groping movements, sometimes stumbling, sometimes making mistakes of a tactical nature—with either too much anti-Americanism or too much fear of offending or alienating "public opinion." Most important, their motivating ideologies are neither socialism—Marxian or otherwise—nor liberalism, although they combine elements of both. Rather, the ideology of both the *Barbudos* ["bearded ones" in Spanish] of Cuba and the campus revolutionaries is a refreshing combination of humanism and rationalism. The Fidelista [supporter of Fidel Castro] *knows* the meaning of misery and exploitation, of disease and illiteracy, of unemployment and squalor in the midst of plenty, of graft and corruption—he has lived it; the campus rebel, lacking the Cuban experience, nonetheless *feels* it—it violates his sense of values. The Fidelista understands the ailments of Cuba—and of Guatemala, Haiti, the Dominican Republic, and all the remaining "hungry nations"—and he intends to translate this knowledge into action. In at least one sense the Fidelista is very fortunate. He is confronted with the opportunity to steer Cuba's, and perhaps Latin America's, destiny upon the path which he chooses. So he sets about, rationally, to build a new society. Many students at U. of C., Stanford, San Francisco and San Jose State Colleges, at Wisconsin, and Chicago and NYU [New York University] grasp and appreciate this attempt to direct human history, to take hold of one's environment and shape it, to institutionalize the better human values. These students also recognize the dangers involved, both for themselves and the Cubans. They would oppose both American intervention and totalitarianism in the name of Cuban nationalism or socialism, but they are not without understanding for revolutionary excesses.

There are also, of course, important differences between the Cuban and campus rebels. The former are united, sure of themselves and where they are going. The latter, though often united on specific issues, are divided over basic questions, hesitant, and with no permanent goals or direction.

No all-inclusive term adequately characterizes the range of ideologies which influence the campus rebels. While such a characterization might fairly represent the convictions of one subgroup, it would radically conflict with those of another. The link which binds the various tendencies within the student movement is a firm belief in the value and necessity of *active dissent*. In the course of its short existence, the campus revolution has forged an ideology of dissent which sustains its adherents during the thick of political action and in some sense represents a compromise between the opposing trends of individualism and mass action. . . .

The old left is dead. . . . Contemporary "liberalism" is impotent; and no longer even *is* liberalism in our sense. We are tired of the stereotyped responses of the Marxist, and disgusted with the liberal's rhetoric, agnosticism, and incapacity for political action. We are radical, but disregard the orthodoxy of Marxism. We are liberal, but not tied to the status quo. In a sense we are eclectic, willing to accept the best of both philosophies. . . .

In a sense we are lost, for we do drift about in rough and uncharted seas. We are fearful that if we do establish a steady course it may take us somewhere we do not want to go. We also know that the huge waves tossed up from the depths of conservative tradition and state authority may weaken, or even destroy us.

Perhaps this is why we have only a dissenting ideology. We unhesitantly express what we are against, but are less sure of what we are for. Because of this, we are rather more reformist than revolutionary. We tend to believe in nonviolence not only because it is effective, but also because it is inherently good. . . .

Postscript: The American intervention in Cuba [Bay of Pigs], undertaken after this communication was in print, has had a tremendous impact on both the size of the student movement and its ideology, at least in the Bay Area. Many student "hangers-on" and potential rebels have been activated by the gross nature of the irrationality in high places. Most important, however, is the fact that U.S. imperialistic ventures have served to *radicalize* the dissenters. For example: (a) the concept of demonstration has been altered to include "dramatic nonviolent acts of civil disobedience"; (b) new and truly radical students have gained leadership positions and the old activists have moved to the left along with their student base of support.

10

FANNIE LOU HAMER

Remembering 1962

1977

Fannie Lou Hamer was a forty-two-year-old plantation worker in Sun-flower County, in the Mississippi Delta. She joined a voter registration campaign in 1962 and became a leader of SNCC and the Mississippi Freedom Democratic party (MFDP). In this oral history, Mrs. Hamer describes how she came into the movement and the retribution she faced for attempting to register to vote.

Well, we were living on a plantation about four and a half miles east of here. . . . Pap had been out there thirty years, and I had been out there eighteen years, 'cause we had been married at that time eighteen years. And you know, things were just rough. . . . I don't think that I ever remember working for as much as four dollars a day. Yes, one year I remember working for four dollars a day, and I was gettin' as much as the men, 'cause I kept up with the time. . . . But anyway, I just knowed things wasn't right.

So then that was in 1962 when the civil rights workers came into this county. Now, I didn't know anything about voter registration or nothin' like that, 'cause people had never been told that they could register to vote. And livin' out in the country, if you had a little radio, by the time you got in at night, you'd be too tired to listen at what was goin' on. . . . So they had a rally. I had gone to church that Sunday, and

Fannie Lou Hamer, "Remembering 1962," in Howell Raines, *My Soul Is Rested: Movement Days in the Deep South Remembered* (1977; repr., New York: Penguin Books, 1983), 249–52.

the minister announced that they were gon' have a mass meeting that Monday night. Well, I didn't know what a mass meeting was, and I was just curious to go to a mass meeting. So I did . . . and they was talkin' about how blacks had a right to register and how they had a right to *vote.* . . . Just listenin' at 'em, I could just see myself votin' people outa office that I know was wrong and didn't do nothin' to help the poor. I said, you know, that's sumpin' I really wanna be involved in, and finally at the end of that rally, I had made up my mind that I was gonna come out there when they said you could go down that Friday to try to register.

She remembers the date precisely: August 31, 1962. She and seventeen others climbed aboard an old bus owned by a black man from neighboring Bolivar County. SNCC had chartered it for the thirty-mile ride to the county seat in Indianola. Once there, she was the first into the registrar's office.

. . . He brought a big old book out there, and he gave me the sixteenth section of the Constitution of Mississippi, and that was dealing with de facto laws, and I didn't know nothin' about no de facto laws, didn't know nothin' about any of 'em. I could copy it like it was in the book . . . but after I got through copying it, he told me to give a reasonable interpretation and tell the meaning of that section that I had copied. Well, I flunked out. . . .

So then we started back to Ruleville and on our way back to Ruleville, this same highway patrolman that I had seen steady cruisin' around this bus stopped us. We had crossed that bridge, coming over from Indianola. They got out the cars, flagged the bus down. When they flagged the bus down, they told all of us to get off the bus. So at this time, we just started singing "Have a Little Talk with Jesus," and we got off the bus, and all they wanted then was for us to get back on the bus. They arrested Bob [Moses][1] and told the bus driver he was under arrest. So we went back then to Indianola. The bus driver was fined one hundred dollars for driving a bus with too much yellow in it. Now ain't that ridiculous?

[Interviewer:] For what?

Too much yellow. Said the bus looked too much like a school bus. That's funny, but it's the truth. But you see, it was to frighten us to

[1]Bob Moses was the first SNCC organizer in Mississippi, initiating a voter registration project in late 1961. Known for his selflessness, he became a revered figure in the movement.

death. This same bus had been used year after year hauling cotton choppers and cotton pickers to Florida to try to make a livin' that winter, and he had never been arrested before. But the day he tried . . . to carry us to Indianola, they fined him a hundred dollars, and I guess it was so ridiculous that they finally cut the fine down to thirty dollars, and all of us *together*—not one, but all of us together—had enough to pay the fine. So we paid the fine, and then we got back on the bus and come on to Ruleville.

So Rev. Jeff Summers, who live on Charles Street, just the next street over, he carried me out there on the Marlowe Plantation where I had worked for eighteen years. And when I got out there, my little girl—she's dead now, Dorothy—she met me and one of Pap's cousins, and said that man [who owned the plantation] had been raising a lot of Cain ever since we left, that he had been in the field more times than he usually come a day, because I had gone to the courthouse. See, the people at the courthouse would call and tell it. So they was kinda scared, and quite natural I began to feel nervous, but I knowed I hadn't done nothin' wrong. So after my little girl told me, wasn't too long 'fore Pap got off, and he was tellin' me the same thing that the other kids had told me.

I went on in the house, and I sat down on a little old bed that belonged to the little girl, and when I sat down on the bed, this man [who owned the plantation] he come up and he asked Pap, "Did you tell Fannie Lou what I said?" And Pap said, "Yessir, I sho' did." And I got up and walked to the door, and then he asked me, "Did Pap tell you what I said?" I said, "He told me." And he said, "I mean that. You'll have to go back to Indianola and withdraw, or you have to leave this place." So I said, "Mr. Dee, I didn't go down there to register for you. I went down there to register for myself." And that made him madder, you know.

So he told me, "I want your answer now, yea or nay." And he said, "They gon'"—now, I don't know who the *they* were, whether it was the white Citizens Council or the Ku Klux Klan, 'cause I don't think one is no worse than the other—"they gon' worry me tonight. They gon' worry the hell outa me, and I'm gon' worry hell outa you. You got 'til in the mornin' to tell me. But if you don't go back there and withdraw, you got to leave the plantation."

So I knowed I wasn't goin' back to withdraw, so wasn't nothin' for me to do but leave the plantation. So Pap brought me out that same night and I come to Mrs. Tucker's, a lady live over on Byron Street. I went to her house, and I stayed, and Pap began to feel nervous when he went to the shop and saw some buckshot shells. And they don't have buckshot shells to *play* with in August and September, because you ain't huntin' or nothin' like that.

On September tenth—again she recalls the date precisely—came the nightrider attack. . . . The riders shot into the McDonald home, where the SNCC workers were staying, and into the Tucker home, where Mrs. Hamer had been given shelter. "They shot in that house sixteen times, tryin' to kill me," she remembers. She fled to the home of a niece in Tallahatchie County when the nighttime terrorism continued on into the fall.

I stayed away, 'cause things then—you could see 'em at night. They would have fires in the middle of the road. . . . You wouldn't see no Klan signs, but just make a fire in the middle of the road. And it was *so dangerous,* I stayed in Tallahatchie County all of September and then October, and then November I come back to Ruleville. I was comin', I didn't know why I was comin', but I was just sick of runnin' and hadn't done nothin'. . . . I started tryin' to find a place to stay, 'cause we didn't have nothin'.

The woman who had been her sixth-grade school teacher put her in touch with a black woman who had a three-room house for rent "for eighteen dollars a month and that was a lotta money." She and her family moved in on December 3.

That was on a Sunday, and that Monday, the fourth of December, I went back to Indianola to the circuit clerk's office and I told him who I was and I was there to take that literacy test again.

I said, "Now, you cain't have me fired 'cause I'm already fired, and I won't have to move now, because I'm not livin' in no white man's house." I said, "I'll be here every thirty days until I become a registered voter." 'Cause that's what you would have to do: go every thirty days and see had you passed the literacy test. . . . I went back then the tenth of January in 1963, and I had become registered. . . .

11

TOM HAYDEN AND STUDENTS FOR A DEMOCRATIC SOCIETY

The Port Huron Statement

August 1962

The Port Huron Statement identifies the "new" in New Left with a new generation, which was key to the appeal of Students for a Democratic Society (SDS). Its principal author was Tom Hayden, a University of Michigan student who had gone to Mississippi in 1961 to report on SNCC's voter registration project. Students at colleges such as Harvard, Oberlin, Swarthmore, Michigan, and the University of Texas joined SDS because of the wide-ranging intellectual vision of The Port Huron Statement, which fused Marxism, liberalism, and religious idealism. The organization became a training ground for young New Left leaders such as Hayden, who honed their speaking, writing, and debating skills there.

Introduction: Agenda for a Generation

We are people of this generation, bred in at least modest comfort, housed now in universities, looking uncomfortably to the world we inherit.

When we were kids the United States was the wealthiest and strongest country in the world; the only one with the atom bomb, the least scarred by modern war, an initiator of the United Nations that we thought would distribute Western influence throughout the world. Freedom and equality for each individual, government of, by, and for the people—these American values we found good, principles by which we could live as men. Many of us began maturing in complacency.

As we grew, however, our comfort was penetrated by events too troubling to dismiss. First, the permeating and victimizing fact of human degradation, symbolized by the Southern struggle against racial bigotry, compelled most of us from silence to activism. Second,

Reprinted in Paul Jacobs and Saul Landau, eds., *The New Radicals: A Report with Documents* (New York: Vintage, 1966), 150–56.

the enclosing fact of the Cold War, symbolized by the presence of the Bomb, brought awareness that we ourselves, and our friends, and millions of abstract "others" we knew more directly because of our common peril, might die at any time. We might deliberately ignore, or avoid, or fail to feel all other human problems, but not these two, for these were too immediate and crushing in their impact, too challenging in the demand that we as individuals take the responsibility for encounter and resolution. . . .

Not only did tarnish appear on our image of American virtue, not only did disillusion occur when the hypocrisy of American ideals was discovered, but we began to sense that what we had originally seen as the American Golden Age was actually the decline of an era. The worldwide outbreak of revolution against colonialism and imperialism, the entrenchment of totalitarian states, the menace of war, overpopulation, international disorder, supertechnology—these trends were testing the tenacity of our own commitment to democracy and freedom and our abilities to visualize their application to a world in upheaval.

Our work is guided by the sense that we may be the last generation in the experiment with living. But we are a minority—the vast majority of our people regard the temporary equilibriums of our society and world as eternally functional parts. In this is perhaps the outstanding paradox: we ourselves are imbued with urgency, yet the message of our society is that there is no viable alternative to the present. Beneath the reassuring tones of the politicians, beneath the common opinion that America will "muddle through," beneath the stagnation of those who have closed their minds to the future, is the pervading feeling that there simply are no alternatives, that our times have witnessed the exhaustion not only of Utopias, but of any new departures as well. Feeling the press of complexity upon the emptiness of life, people are fearful of the thought that at any moment things might be thrust out of control. They fear change itself, since change might smash whatever invisible framework seems to hold back chaos for them now. For most Americans, all crusades are suspect, threatening. . . .

Values

. . . We regard *men*[1] as infinitely precious and possessed of unfulfilled capacities for reason, freedom, and love. In affirming these principles

---

[1]Prior to the women's liberation movement, writers and speakers routinely used "man" or "men" to mean all people.

we are aware of countering perhaps the dominant conceptions of man in the twentieth century: that he is a thing to be manipulated, and that he is inherently incapable of directing his own affairs. We oppose the depersonalization that reduces human beings to the status of things— if anything, the brutalities of the twentieth century teach that means and ends are intimately related, that vague appeals to "posterity" cannot justify the mutilations of the present. . . .

We would replace power rooted in possession, privilege, or circumstance by power and uniqueness rooted in love, reflectiveness, reason, and creativity. As a *social system* we seek the establishment of a democracy of individual participation, governed by two central aims: that the individual share in those social decisions determining the quality and direction of his life; that society be organized to encourage independence in men and provide the media for their common participation.

In a participatory democracy, the political life would be based in several root principles:

that decision-making of basic social consequence be carried on by public groupings;

that politics be seen positively, as the art of collectively creating an acceptable pattern of social relations;

that politics has the function of bringing people out of isolation and into community, thus being a necessary, though not sufficient, means of finding meaning in personal life;

that the political order should serve to clarify problems in a way instrumental to their solution; it should provide outlets for the expression of personal grievance and aspiration; opposing views should be organized so as to illuminate choices and facilitate the attainment of goals; channels should be commonly available to relate men to knowledge and to power so that private problems—from bad recreation facilities to personal alienation—are formulated as general issues. . . .

12

BETTY FRIEDAN

The Feminine Mystique
1963

*During the 1960s, Betty Friedan personified the growing anger of edu-
cated women. Her 1963 bestseller,* The Feminine Mystique, *from which
this selection is excerpted, helped revive feminism as a national movement. Friedan had a leftist background as a journalist for a Communist-
led trade union in the 1940s, but she kept that history quiet. The renown
that came with her book made Friedan the natural first president of the
National Organization for Women (NOW) in 1966. Since then, some historians have criticized her for exaggerating the "mystique" and have
pointed out that many women's organizations had continued fighting for
equality during the 1950s. Some critics have noted that Friedan wrote
mainly about white middle-class women. Yet for all the criticism,* The
Feminine Mystique, *one of the most effective indictments of oppression
in U.S. history, has sold more than a million copies and still remains in
print.*

. . . The problem lay buried, unspoken, for many years in the minds of
American women. It was a strange stirring, a sense of dissatisfaction, a
yearning that women suffered in the middle of the twentieth century
in the United States. Each suburban wife struggled with it alone. As
she made the beds, shopped for groceries, matched slipcover material, ate peanut butter sandwiches with her children, chauffeured Cub
Scouts and Brownies, lay beside her husband at night—she was
afraid to ask even of herself the silent question—"Is this all?"

For over fifteen years there was no word of this yearning in the millions of words written about women, for women, in all the columns,
books and articles by experts telling women their role was to seek fulfillment as wives and mothers. Over and over women heard in voices
of tradition and of Freudian sophistication that they could desire no

Betty Friedan, *The Feminine Mystique* (New York: W. W. Norton, 1963), 15–20.

greater destiny than to glory in their own femininity. Experts told them how to catch a man and keep him, how to breastfeed children and handle their toilet training, how to cope with sibling rivalry and adolescent rebellion; how to buy a dishwasher, bake bread, cook gourmet snails, and build a swimming pool with their own hands; how to dress, look, and act more feminine and make marriage more exciting; how to keep their husbands from dying young and their sons from growing into delinquents. They were taught to pity the neurotic, unfeminine, unhappy women who wanted to be poets or physicists or presidents. They learned that truly feminine women do not want careers, higher education, political rights—the independence and the opportunities that the old-fashioned feminists fought for. Some women, in their forties and fifties, still remembered painfully giving up those dreams, but most of the younger women no longer even thought about them. A thousand expert voices applauded their femininity, their adjustment, their new maturity. All they had to do was devote their lives from earliest girlhood to finding a husband and bearing children.

By the end of the nineteen-fifties, the average marriage age of women in America dropped to 20, and was still dropping, into the teens. Fourteen million girls were engaged by 17. The proportion of women attending college in comparison with men dropped from 47 per cent in 1920 to 35 per cent in 1958. A century earlier, women had fought for higher education; now girls went to college to get a husband. By the mid-fifties, 60 per cent dropped out of college to marry, or because they were afraid too much education would be a marriage bar. Colleges built dormitories for "married students," but the students were almost always the husbands. A new degree was instituted for the wives—"Ph.T." (Putting Husband Through).

Then American girls began getting married in high school. And the women's magazines, deploring the unhappy statistics about these young marriages, urged that courses on marriage, and marriage counselors, be installed in the high schools. Girls started going steady at twelve and thirteen, in junior high. Manufacturers put out brassieres with false bosoms of foam rubber for little girls of ten. And an advertisement for a child's dress, sizes 3–6x, in the *New York Times* in the fall of 1960, said: "She Too Can Join the Man-Trap Set."

By the end of the fifties, the United States birthrate was overtaking India's. The birth-control movement, renamed Planned Parenthood, was asked to find a method whereby women who had been advised that a third or fourth baby would be born dead or defective might have it anyhow. Statisticians were especially astounded at the fantastic increase in the number of babies among college women. Where once they had two children, now they had four, five, six. Women who had once wanted careers were now making careers out of having babies. So rejoiced *Life* magazine in a 1956 paean to the movement of American women back to the home.

In a New York hospital, a woman had a nervous breakdown when she found she could not breastfeed her baby. In other hospitals, women dying of cancer refused a drug which research had proved might save their lives: its side effects were said to be unfeminine. "If I have only one life, let me live it as a blonde," a larger-than-life-sized picture of a pretty, vacuous woman proclaimed from newspaper, magazine, and drugstore ads. And across America, three out of every ten women dyed their hair blonde. They ate a chalk called Metrecal, instead of food, to shrink to the size of the thin young models. Department-store buyers reported that American women, since 1939, had become three and four sizes smaller. "Women are out to fit the clothes, instead of vice-versa," one buyer said.

Interior decorators were designing kitchens with mosaic murals and original paintings, for kitchens were once again the center of women's lives. Home sewing became a million-dollar industry. Many women no longer left their homes, except to shop, chauffeur their children, or attend a social engagement with their husbands. Girls were growing up in America without ever having jobs outside the home. In the late fifties, a sociological phenomenon was suddenly remarked: a third of American women now worked, but most were no longer young and very few were pursuing careers. They were married women who held part-time jobs, selling or secretarial, to put their husbands through school, their sons through college, or to help pay the mortgage. Or they were widows supporting families. Fewer and fewer women were entering professional work. The shortages in the nursing, social work, and teaching professions caused crises in almost every American city. Concerned over the Soviet Union's lead in the space race, scientists noted that America's greatest source of unused brainpower was women. But girls would not study physics: it was "unfeminine." A girl refused a science fellowship at Johns Hopkins to take a job in a real-estate office. All she wanted, she said, was what every other American girl wanted—to get married, have four children and live in a nice house in a nice suburb.

The suburban housewife—she was the dream image of the young American women and the envy, it was said, of women all over the world. The American housewife—freed by science and labor-saving appliances from the drudgery, the dangers of childbirth and the illnesses of her grandmother. She was healthy, beautiful, educated, concerned only about her husband, her children, her home. She had found true feminine fulfillment. As a housewife and mother, she was respected as a full and equal partner to man in his world. She was free to choose automobiles, clothes, appliances, supermarkets; she had everything that women ever dreamed of.

In the fifteen years after World War II, this mystique of feminine fulfillment became the cherished and self-perpetuating core of contemporary American culture. Millions of women lived their lives in the image of those pretty pictures of the American suburban housewife, kissing their husbands goodbye in front of the picture window, depositing their stationwagonsful of children at school, and smiling as they ran the new electric waxer over the spotless kitchen floor. They baked their own bread, sewed their own and their children's clothes, kept their new washing machines and dryers running all day. They changed the sheets on the beds twice a week instead of once, took the rug-hooking class in adult education, and pitied their poor frustrated mothers, who had dreamed of having a career. Their only dream was to be perfect wives and mothers; their highest ambition to have five children and a beautiful house, their only fight to get and keep their husbands. They had no thought for the unfeminine problems of the world outside the home; they wanted the men to make the major decisions. They gloried in their role as women, and wrote proudly on the census blank: "Occupation: housewife."

For over fifteen years, the words written for women, and the words women used when they talked to each other, while their husbands sat on the other side of the room and talked shop or politics or septic tanks, were about problems with their children, or how to keep their husbands happy, or improve their children's school, or cook chicken or make slipcovers. Nobody argued whether women were inferior or superior to men; they were simply different. Words like "emancipation" and "career" sounded strange and embarrassing; no one had used them for years. When a Frenchwoman named Simone de Beauvoir wrote a book called *The Second Sex,* an American critic commented that she obviously "didn't know what life was all about," and besides, she was talking about French women. The "woman problem" in America no longer existed.

If a woman had a problem in the 1950's and 1960's, she knew that something must be wrong with her marriage, or with herself. Other women were satisfied with their lives, she thought. What kind of a woman was she if she did not feel this mysterious fulfillment waxing the kitchen floor? She was so ashamed to admit her dissatisfaction that she never knew how many other women shared it. If she tried to tell her husband, he didn't understand what she was talking about. She did not really understand it herself. For over fifteen years women in America found it harder to talk about this problem than about sex. Even the psychoanalysts had no name for it. When a woman went to a psychiatrist for help, as many women did, she would say, "I'm so ashamed," or "I must be hopelessly neurotic." "I don't know what's wrong with women today," a suburban psychiatrist said uneasily. "I only know something is wrong because most of my patients happen to be women. And their problem isn't sexual." Most women with this problem did not go to see a psychoanalyst, however. "There's nothing wrong really," they kept telling themselves. "There isn't any problem."

But on an April morning in 1959, I heard a mother of four, having coffee with four other mothers in a suburban development fifteen miles from New York, say in a tone of quiet desperation, "the problem." And the others knew, without words, that she was not talking about a problem with her husband, or her children, or her home. Suddenly they realized they all shared the same problem, the problem that has no name. They began, hesitantly, to talk about it. Later, after they had picked up their children at nursery school and taken them home to nap, two of the women cried, in sheer relief, just to know they were not alone.

13

MARTIN LUTHER KING JR.

Letter from Birmingham Jail

April 16, 1963

The campaign that SCLC initiated in Birmingham, Alabama, in the spring of 1963 was the climax of the civil rights movement in the South. It forced President Kennedy finally to commit to a major civil rights bill. It was also a test of Martin Luther King's leadership. By 1963, some

Reprinted in Thomas C. Holt and Elsa Barkley Brown, ed., *Major Problems in African-American History: Volume II: From Freedom to "Freedom Now," 1865–1990s* (Boston: Houghton Mifflin, 2000), 289–90.

activists were frustrated by how the national press focused on him and ignored local leaders. This open letter left little doubt of King's radical commitment. It was handwritten in jail, in response to an advertisement from white clergy asking King to shut down the highly disruptive campaign. Though cited less often than his "I Have a Dream" speech, delivered in August 1963 during the March on Washington, it is a better reflection of King's politics and his refusal to wait any longer for justice. It had a profound effect on many white Christians in the North.

My Dear Fellow Clergymen:

While confined here in the Birmingham city jail, I came across your recent statement calling my present activities "unwise and untimely." . . .

You deplore the demonstrations taking place in Birmingham. But your statement, I am sorry to say, fails to express a similar concern for the conditions that brought about the demonstrations. . . . It is unfortunate that demonstrations are taking place in Birmingham, but it is even more unfortunate that the city's white power structure left the Negro community with no alternative. . . .

One of the basic points in your statement is that the action that I and my associates have taken in Birmingham is untimely. . . .

. . . Frankly, I have yet to engage in a direct-action campaign that was "well timed" in the view of those who have not suffered unduly from the disease of segregation. For years now I have heard the word "Wait!" It rings in the ear of every Negro with piercing familiarity. . . .

We have waited for more than 340 years for our constitutional and God-given rights. The nations of Asia and Africa are moving with jet-like speed toward gaining political independence, but we still creep at horse-and-buggy pace toward gaining a cup of coffee at a lunch counter. Perhaps it is easy for those who have never felt the stinging darts of segregation to say, "Wait." But when you have seen vicious mobs lynch your mothers and fathers at will and drown your sisters and brothers at whim; when you have seen hate-filled policemen curse, kick and even kill your black brothers and sisters; when you see the vast majority of your twenty million Negro brothers smothering in an airtight cage of poverty in the midst of an affluent society; when you suddenly find your tongue twisted and your speech stammering as you seek to explain to your six-year-old daughter why she can't go to the public amusement park that has just been advertised on television, and see tears welling up in her eyes when she is told that Funtown is closed to colored children and see ominous clouds of inferiority beginning to form in her little mental sky, and see her beginning to distort her personality by developing an unconscious bitterness toward white people; ... when your first name becomes "nigger," your middle name becomes "boy" (however old you are) and your last name becomes "John," and your wife and mother are never given the respected title "Mrs."; ... when you are forever fighting a degenerating sense of "nobodiness"—then you will understand why we find it difficult to wait. ...

You express a great deal of anxiety over our willingness to break laws. This is certainly a legitimate concern. Since we so diligently urge people to obey the Supreme Court's decision of 1954 outlawing segregation in the public schools, at first glance it may seem rather paradoxical for us consciously to break laws. ... One has not only a legal but a moral responsibility to obey just laws. Conversely, one has a moral responsibility to disobey unjust laws. ...

... All segregation statutes are unjust because segregation distorts the soul and damages the personality. It gives the segregator a false sense of superiority and the segregated a false sense of inferiority. ... [S]egregation is not only politically, economically and sociologically unsound, it is morally wrong and sinful. ...

... A law is unjust if it is inflicted on a minority that, as a result of being denied the right to vote, had no part in enacting or devising the law. ... Throughout Alabama all sorts of devious methods are used to prevent Negroes from becoming registered voters, and there are some counties in which, even though Negroes constitute a majority of the population, not a single Negro is registered. Can any law enacted under such circumstances be considered democratically structured? ...

... You warmly commended the Birmingham police force for keeping "order" and "preventing violence." I doubt that you would have so warmly commended the police force if you had seen its dogs sinking their teeth into unarmed, nonviolent Negroes. ...

It is true that the police have exercised a degree of discipline in handling the demonstrators. In this sense they have conducted themselves rather "nonviolently" in public. But for what purpose? To preserve the evil system of segregation. ...

I wish you had commended the Negro sit-inners and demonstrators of Birmingham for their sublime courage, their willingness to suffer and their amazing discipline in the midst of great provocation. One day the South will recognize its real heroes. They will be the James Merediths, with the noble sense of purpose that enables them to face jeering and hostile mobs. ... They will be old, oppressed, battered Negro women, ... who rose up with a sense of dignity and with [their] people decided not to ride segregated buses. . . . They will be the young high school and college students, the young ministers of the gospel and a host of their elders, courageously and nonviolently sitting in at lunch counters and willingly going to jail for conscience' sake. One day the South will know that when these disinherited children of God sat down at lunch counters, they were in reality standing up for what is best in the American dream and for the most sacred values in our Judaeo-Christian heritage. . . .

Yours for the cause of Peace and Brotherhood,
Martin Luther King Jr.

14

JOHN LEWIS

Wake Up America!

August 28, 1963

SNCC *Chairman John Lewis's speech at the March on Washington provoked a confrontation between cold war liberalism and the civil rights movement. Washington's Catholic archbishop and white union leaders threatened to boycott the march if Lewis criticized President Kennedy, and the speech was edited just before he delivered it. This is the speech Lewis wrote that was released to the press before he took out the criticisms of the Kennedy administration. Even toned down, it contained a revolutionary call for the destruction of white supremacy. Lewis's anger at Kennedy's unwillingness to make the FBI protect civil rights organizers and his disgust with both political parties anticipated Black Power. At the time, white and black moderates hailed the march as a triumph, but many younger activists agreed with Malcolm X, who labeled it the "Farce in Washington," and believed the movement was being co-opted by Kennedy. Lewis was elected to Congress in 1986 and has become a senior member of the Democratic leadership there.*

Reprinted in Thomas C. Holt and Elsa Barkley Brown, eds., *Major Problems in African-American History: Volume II: From Freedom to "Freedom Now," 1865–1990s* (Boston: Houghton Mifflin, 2000), 291–92.

We march today for jobs and freedom, but we have nothing to be proud of. For hundreds and thousands of our brothers are not here. They have no money for their transportation, for they are receiving starvation wages ... or no wages, at all.

In good conscience, we cannot support the administration's civil rights bill, for it is too little, and too late. There's not one thing in the bill that will protect our people from police brutality.

This bill will not protect young children and old women from police dogs and fire hoses, [when] engaging in peaceful demonstrations. ...

The voting section of this bill will not help thousands of black citizens who want to vote. It will not help the citizens of Mississippi, of Alabama, and Georgia, who are qualified to vote, but lack a 6th Grade education. "One man, one vote," is the African cry. It is ours, too. (It must be ours.) ...

We are now involved in ... revolution. This nation is still a place of cheap political leaders who build their careers on immoral compromise and ally themselves with open forms of political, economic and social exploitation. What political leader here can stand up and say, "My party is the party of principles"? The party of Kennedy is also the party of Eastland. The party of Javits is also the party of Goldwater.[1] Where is *our* party?

In some parts of the South we work in the fields from sun-up to sundown for $12 a week. In Albany, Georgia, nine of our leaders have been indicted not by Dixiecrats but by the Federal Government for peaceful protest.[2] But what did the Federal Government do when Albany's Deputy Sheriff beat Attorney C. B. King and left him half dead? What did the Federal Government do when local police officials kicked and assaulted the pregnant wife of Slater King, and she lost her baby?

It seems to me that the Albany indictment is part of a conspiracy on the part of the Federal Government and local politicians in the interest of expediency.

---

[1]Senator James Eastland (D-Miss.) was a well-known segregationist. Senator Jacob Javits (R-N.Y.) was one of the strongest civil rights supporters in the Senate. Senator Barry Goldwater (R-Ariz.), already a favorite for the Republican presidential nomination in 1964, had stated that legislation such as the Civil Rights Act was unconstitutional.

[2]In 1962, SNCC and SCLC began a joint campaign in Albany, Georgia, that resulted in a bitter defeat for the civil rights movement. The Dixiecrats, formally known as the States' Rights Democratic Party, were a group of southern Democrats who walked out of the 1948 Democratic Convention when the party took a pro–civil rights position. They ran South Carolina governor Strom Thurmond for president, and he carried four states where he was the only "Democrat" listed on the ballot. After that, the term was widely used to describe the Democrats' diehard segregationist wing.

I want to know, which side is the Federal Government on?

The revolution is at hand, and we must free ourselves of the chains of political and economic slavery. The non-violent revolution is saying, "We will not wait for the courts to act, for we have been waiting for hundreds of years. We will not wait for the President, the Justice Department, nor Congress, but we will take matters into our own hands and create a source of power, outside any national structure that could and would assure us a victory." To those who have said, "Be Patient and Wait," we must say that, "Patience is a dirty and nasty word." We cannot be patient, we do not want to be free gradually, we want our freedom, and we want it now. We cannot depend on any political party, for both the Democrats and the Republicans have betrayed the basic principles of the Declaration of Independence.

We all recognize the fact that if any radical social, political and economic changes are to take place in our society, the people, the masses, must bring them about. In the struggle we must seek more than civil rights; we must work for the community of love, peace and true brotherhood. Our minds, souls, and hearts cannot rest until freedom and justice exist for *all the people.*

The revolution is a serious one. Mr. Kennedy is trying to take the revolution out of the street and put it in the courts. Listen, Mr. Kennedy, listen Mr. Congressman, listen fellow citizens, the black masses are on the march for jobs and freedom, and we must say to the politicians that there won't be a "cooling-off" period. . . .

We won't stop now. All of the forces of Eastland, Barnett, Wallace, and Thurmond won't stop this revolution.[3] The time will come when we will not confine our marching to Washington. We will march through the South, through the Heart of Dixie, the way Sherman did. We shall pursue our own "scorched earth" policy and burn Jim Crow to the ground—nonviolently. We shall fragment the South into a thousand pieces and put them back together in the image of democracy. We will make the action of the past few months look petty. And I say to you, WAKE UP AMERICA!

---

[3]Lewis names some of the most famous segregationist leaders, all Democrats: Governor Ross Barnett of Mississippi; Governor George Wallace of Alabama; Senator Strom Thurmond of South Carolina, who became a Republican in 1964, initiating a massive shift by southern whites.

15

MALCOLM X

Message to the Grassroots
November 10, 1963

Detroit was one of the cities where the Black Power movement began. In November 1963, the Northern Negro Grassroots Leadership Conference convened there with the goal of moving the struggle of African Americans beyond civil rights. Organizers invited Malcolm X, a prominent minister of the Nation of Islam (NOI), to give the keynote speech. The NOI rejected involvement in politics, urging blacks to withdraw from the white world. In the early 1960s, however, Malcolm started talking more and more about political issues. In this widely reproduced speech, he insisted that all true revolutions are violent and cast the African American struggle within a global anticolonial revolution. Even activists deeply committed to the nonviolent, interracial civil rights movement were shaken and inspired by his rhetoric.

We want to have just an off-the-cuff chat between you and me, us. We want to talk right down to earth in a language that everybody here can easily understand. We all agree tonight, all of the speakers have agreed, that America has a very serious problem. Not only does America have a very serious problem, but our people have a very serious problem. America's problem is us. We're her problem. The only reason she has a problem is she doesn't want us here. And every time you look at yourself, be you black, brown, red or yellow, a so-called Negro, you represent a person who poses such a serious problem for America because you're not wanted. Once you face this as a fact, then you can start plotting a course that will make you appear intelligent, instead of unintelligent.

What you and I need to do is learn to forget our differences. When we come together, we don't come together as Baptists or Methodists. You don't catch hell because you're a Baptist, and you don't catch hell

Reprinted in George Breitman, ed., *Malcolm X Speaks: Selected Speeches and Statements* (New York: Grove Weidenfeld, 1966), 4–17.

because you're a Methodist. You don't catch hell because you're a Methodist or Baptist, you don't catch hell because you're a Democrat or a Republican, you don't catch hell because you're a Mason or an Elk, and you sure don't catch hell because you're an American; because if you were an American, you wouldn't catch hell. You catch hell because you're a black man. You catch hell, all of us catch hell, for the same reason.

So we're all black people, so-called Negroes, second-class citizens, ex-slaves. You're nothing but an ex-slave. You don't like to be told that. But what else are you? You are ex-slaves. You didn't come here on the "Mayflower." You came here on a slave ship. In chains, like a horse, or a cow, or a chicken. And you were brought here by the people who came here on the "Mayflower," you were brought here by the so-called Pilgrims, or Founding Fathers. They were the ones who brought you here.

We have a common enemy. We have this in common: We have a common oppressor, a common exploiter, and a common discriminator. But once we all realize that we have a common enemy, then we unite—on the basis of what we have in common. And what we have foremost in common is that enemy—the white man. He's an enemy to all of us. I know some of you all think that some of them aren't enemies. Time will tell. . . .

Instead of airing our differences in public, we have to realize we're all the same family. And when you have a family squabble, you don't get out on the sidewalk. If you do, everybody calls you uncouth, unrefined, uncivilized, savage. If you don't make it at home, you settle it at home; you get in the closet, argue it out behind closed doors, and then when you come out on the street, you pose a common front, a united front. And this is what we need to do in the community, and in the city, and in the state. We need to stop airing our differences in front of the white man, put the white man out of our meetings, and then sit down and talk shop with each other. That's what we've got to do.

I would like to make a few comments concerning the difference between the black revolution and the Negro revolution. Are they both the same? And if they're not, what is the difference? What is the difference between a black revolution and a Negro revolution? First, what is a revolution? Sometimes I'm inclined to believe that many of our people are using this word "revolution" loosely, without taking careful consideration of what this word actually means, and what its historic characteristics are. When you study the historic nature of revolutions, the motive of a revolution, the objective of a revolution, the result of a revolution, and the methods used in a revolution, you may change words. You may devise another program, you may change your goal and you may change your mind.

Look at the American Revolution in 1776. That revolution was for what? For land. Why did they want land? Independence. How was it carried out? Bloodshed. Number one, it was based on land, the basis of independence. And the only way they could get it was bloodshed. The French Revolution—what was it based on? The landless against the landlord. What was it for? Land. How did they get it? Bloodshed. Was no love lost, was no compromise, was no negotiation. I'm telling you—you don't know what a revolution is. Because when you find out what it is, you'll get back in the alley, you'll get out of the way.

The Russian Revolution—what was it based on? Land; the landless against the landlord. How did they bring it about? Bloodshed. You haven't got a revolution that doesn't involve bloodshed. And you're afraid to bleed. I said, you're afraid to bleed.

As long as the white man sent you to Korea, you bled. He sent you to Germany, you bled. He sent you to the South Pacific to fight the Japanese, you bled. You bleed for white people, but when it comes to seeing your own churches being bombed and little black girls murdered,[1] you haven't got any blood. You bleed when the white man says bleed; you bite when the white man says bite; and you bark when the white man says bark. I hate to say this about us, but it's true. How are you going to be nonviolent in Mississippi, as violent as you were in Korea? How can you justify being nonviolent in Mississippi and Alabama, when your churches are being bombed, and your little girls are being murdered, and at the same time you are going to get violent with Hitler, and [World War II Japanese leader Hideki] Tojo, and somebody else you don't even know?

If violence is wrong in America, violence is wrong abroad. If it is wrong to be violent defending black women and black children and black babies and black men, then it is wrong for America to draft us and make us violent abroad in defense of her. And if it is right for America to draft us, and teach us how to be violent in defense of her, then it is right for you and me to do whatever is necessary to defend our own people right here in this country. . . .

---

[1]A reference to the Birmingham church bombing that killed four young girls two months earlier.

Of all our studies, history is best qualified to reward our research. And when you see that you've got problems, all you have to do is examine the historic method used all over the world by others who have problems similar to yours. Once you see how they got theirs straight, then you know how you can get yours straight. There's been a revolution, a black revolution, going on in Africa. In Kenya, the Mau Mau were revolutionary; they were the ones brought the word "Uhuru" to the fore.[2] The Mau Mau, they were revolutionary, they believed in scorched earth, they knocked everything aside that got in their way, and their revolution also was based on land, a desire for land. In Algeria, the northern part of Africa, a revolution took place. The Algerians were revolutionists, they wanted land. France offered to let them be integrated into France. They told France, to hell with France, they wanted some land, not some France. And they engaged in a bloody battle.[3]

So I cite these various revolutions, brothers and sisters, to show you that you don't have a peaceful revolution. You don't have a turn-the-other-cheek revolution. There's no such thing as a nonviolent revolution. The only kind of revolution that is nonviolent is the Negro revolution. The only revolution in which the goal is loving your enemy is the Negro revolution. It's the only revolution in which the goal is a desegregated lunch counter, a desegregated theater, a desegregated park, and a desegregated public toilet; you can sit down next to white folks—on the toilet. That's no revolution. . . .

The white man knows what a revolution is. He knows that the black revolution is world-wide in scope and in nature. The black revolution is sweeping Asia, is sweeping Africa, is rearing its head in Latin America. The Cuban Revolution—that's a revolution. They overturned the system. Revolution is in Asia, revolution is in Africa, and the white man is screaming because he sees revolution in Latin America. How do you think he'll react to you when you learn what a real revolution is? You don't know what a revolution is. If you did, you wouldn't use that word. . . .

---

[2] In 1954, the Land and Freedom Army, known as the Mau Mau, began an insurrection against British colonialists in Kenya. The revolt was violently suppressed but eventually led to independence in 1963. *Uhuru* is a Kenyan word meaning "freedom" that was widely adopted by African American activists.

[3] The Algerian National Liberation Front, which rebelled against French colonizers in 1954, finally won independence in 1962 after eight years of brutal warfare.

16

Civil Rights Act of 1964, Title VII
July 2, 1964

The Civil Rights Act of 1964 was the key legislation banning public and private discrimination against African Americans or any other racial, ethnic, or religious minority. For the first time in U.S. history, a federal law made it illegal to exclude someone from a job or a public accommodation (such as a hotel, restaurant, or movie theater) because of how he or she looked or where he or she came from or worshiped. Feminists mobilized to insert the category "sex" (along with race, color, religion, and national origin) into Title VII of the act, which regulates employment. As sections 703–705 indicate, the prohibition on employment discrimination included all the mechanisms through which employers, employment agencies, and unions limited access to good jobs.

Sec. 703. (a) It shall be an unlawful employment practice for an employer—

(1) to fail or refuse to hire or to discharge any individual, or otherwise discriminate against any individual with respect to his compensation, terms, conditions, or privileges of employment, because of such individual's race, color, religion, sex, or national origin; or

(2) to limit, segregate, or classify his employees in any way which would deprive or tend to deprive any individual of employment opportunities or otherwise adversely affect his status as an employee, because of such individual's race, color, religion, sex, or national origin.

(b) It shall be an unlawful employment practice for an employment agency to fail or refuse to refer for employment, or otherwise to discriminate against, any individual because of his race, color, religion, sex, or national origin, or to classify or refer for employment any individual on the basis of his race, color, religion, sex, or national origin.

(c) It shall be an unlawful employment practice for a labor organization—

(1) to exclude or to expel from its membership, or otherwise to discriminate against, any individual because of his race, color, religion, sex, or national origin;

(2) to limit, segregate, or classify its membership, or to classify or fail or refuse to refer for employment any individual, in any way which would deprive or tend to deprive any individual of employment opportunities, or would limit such employment opportunities or otherwise adversely affect his status as an employee or as an applicant for employment, because of such individual's race, color, religion, sex, or national origin; or

(3) to cause or attempt to cause an employer to discriminate against an individual in violation of this section.

(d) It shall be an unlawful employment practice for any employer, labor organization, or joint labor-management committee controlling apprenticeship or other training or retraining, including on-the-job training programs, to discriminate against any individual because of his race, color, religion, sex, or national origin in admission to, or employment in, any program established to provide apprenticeship or other training.

(e) Notwithstanding any other provision of this title . . . it shall not be an unlawful employment practice for an employer to hire and employ employees . . . on the basis of . . . religion, sex, or national origin in those certain instances where religion, sex, or national origin is a bona fide occupational qualification reasonably necessary to the normal operation of that particular business or enterprise. . . .

Sec. 704. (b) It shall be an unlawful employment practice for an employer, labor organization, or employment agency to print or publish or cause to be printed or published any notice or advertisement relating to employment by such an employer or membership in or any classification or referral for employment by such a labor organization, or relating to any classification or referral for employment by such an employment agency, indicating any preference, limitation, specification, or discrimination, based on race, color, religion, sex, or national origin, except that such a notice or advertisement may indicate a preference, limitation, specification, or discrimination based on religion, sex, or national origin when religion, sex, or national origin is a bona fide occupational qualification for employment.

Sec. 705. (a) There is hereby created a Commission to be known as
the Equal Employment Opportunity Commission, which shall be com-
posed of five members, not more than three of whom shall be members of the same political party. Members of the Commission shall be
appointed by the President by and with the advice and consent of the
Senate.

17

SALLY BELFRAGE

Remembering Freedom Summer

1965

In this excerpt from her 1965 book, Freedom Summer, *Sally Belfrage
remembers the tension at the training session for northern volunteers in
Oxford, Ohio, as the news came in that three organizers of the Freedom
Summer Project were missing in Mississippi in 1964. (Their bodies were
found six weeks later after an intensive search ordered by President Johnson.) Her memoir captures the innocence and idealism of the mostly
white students, and the exhaustion and tension endured by movement
veterans such as Bob Moses, who had initiated the original voter registration project in Mississippi in 1961.*

Then Bob Moses, the Director of the Summer Project, came to the
front of the floor. He didn't introduce himself, but somehow one knew
who he was. Everyone had heard a little—that he was twenty-nine,
began in Harlem, had a Master's degree in philosophy from Harvard,
and that he had given up teaching in New York to go South after the
first sit-ins. He had been in Mississippi for three years, and he wore
its uniform: a T-shirt and denim overalls, in the bib of which he
propped his hands. He began as though in the middle of a thought.
"When Mrs. Hamer sang, 'If you miss me from the freedom fight, you

Sally Belfrage, *Freedom Summer* (1965; repr., Charlottesville: University of Virginia
Press, 1990), 9–12.

can't find me nowhere; Come on over to the graveyard, I'll be buried over there . . .' that's true."

Moving up to the stage, he drew a map of Mississippi on a blackboard and patiently, from the beginning, outlined the state's areas and attitudes. The top left segment became the Delta; industry was cotton; power in the Citizens' Councils; and opposition to the movement systematic and calculated, aimed at the leadership (including Moses himself—in 1963, the SNCC worker beside him, Jimmy Travis, was shot in the neck and the shoulder as they rode together in a car outside Greenwood), and at decreasing the Negro population by the expedient of automating the cotton fields, thereby "getting it down to a livable ratio." The segment beneath the Delta was the hill country, mostly poor white farmers who had been organizing since the March on Washington. Amite County, McComb: Klan territory, where violence was indiscriminately aimed at "keeping the nigger in his place" and no one was safe. Five Negroes had been murdered there since December. No indictments.

Mississippi gained texture and dimension on the blackboard. Moses put down the chalk, paused, then looked out at us, his eyes reflective behind horn-rims. When he began again he seemed to be addressing each one separately, though talking to no one at all, just thinking aloud. "When you come South, you bring with you the concern of the country—because the people of the country don't identify with Negroes. The guerrilla war in Mississippi is not much different from that in Vietnam. But when we tried to see President Johnson, his secretary said that Vietnam was popping up all over his calendar and he hadn't time to talk to us." Now, he said, because of the Summer Project, because whites were involved, a crack team of FBI men was going down to Mississippi to investigate. "We have been asking for them for three years. Now the federal government is concerned; there will be more protection for us, and hopefully for the Negroes who live there."

He stood looking at his feet. "Our goals are limited. If we can go and come back alive, then that is something. If you can go into Negro homes and just sit and talk, that will be a huge job. We're not thinking of integrating the lunch counters. The Negroes in Mississippi haven't the money to eat in those places anyway. They still don't dare go into the white half of the integrated bus terminals—they must weigh that against having their houses bombed or losing their jobs."

He stopped again, and everyone waited without a sound. "Mississippi has been called 'The Closed Society.' It is closed, locked. We think the key is in the vote. Any change, any possibility for dissidence and opposition, depends first on a political breakthrough." . . .

There was an interruption then at a side entrance: three or four staff members had come in and were whispering agitatedly. One of them walked over to the stage and sprang up to whisper to Moses, who bent on his knees to hear. In a moment he was alone again. Still crouched, he gazed at the floor at his feet, unconscious of us. Time passed. When he stood and spoke, he was somewhere else; it was simply that he was obliged to say something, but his voice was automatic. "Yesterday morning, three of our people left Meridian, Mississippi, to investigate a church-burning in Neshoba County. They haven't come back, and we haven't had any word from them. We spoke to John Doar in the Justice Department. He promised to order the FBI to act, but the local FBI still says they have been given no authority."

He stood, while activity burst out around him. In the audience, people asked each other who the three were; volunteers who had been at the first week of orientation remembered them. Then a thin girl in shorts was talking to us from the stage: Rita Schwerner, the wife of one of the three.

She paced as she spoke, her eyes distraught and her face quite white, but in a voice that was even and disciplined. It was suddenly clear that she, Moses, and others on the staff had been up all the night before. The three men had been arrested for speeding. Deputy Sheriff Price of Neshoba claimed to have released them at 10 P.M. the same day. All the jails in the area had been checked, with no results. The Jackson FBI office kept saying they were not sure a federal statute had been violated.

Rita asked us to form in groups by home areas and wire our congressmen that the federal government, though begged to investigate, had refused to act, and that if the government did not act, none of us was safe. Someone in the audience asked her to spell the names. . . .

No one was willing to believe that the event involved more than a disappearance. It was hard to believe even that. Somehow it seemed only a climactic object lesson, part of the morning's lecture, an anecdote to give life to the words of Bob Moses. To think of it in other terms was to be forced to identify with the three, to be prepared, irrevocably, to give one's life. . . .

18

MARIO SAVIO

An End to History

November 1964

Mario Savio was a graduate student in philosophy at Berkeley who had participated in the Freedom Summer Project of 1964. His fierce eloquence and the attempts of the university administration to punish him only added to his appeal as the spokesman of the Free Speech Movement (FSM). This impromptu speech, given on the steps of the main administration building when the FSM was at its peak, emphasized what he saw as the danger of students becoming merely "products" of the university, or "well-behaved children." The connection he made between racism in Mississippi and bureaucratic control over students' lives at Berkeley underlines how the new student radicals saw themselves as part of a larger movement for human dignity.

Last summer I went to Mississippi to join the struggle there for civil rights. This fall I am engaged in another phase of the same struggle, this time in Berkeley. The two battlefields may seem quite different to some observers, but this is not the case. The same rights are at stake in both places—the right to participate as citizens in democratic society and the right to due process of law. Further, it is a struggle against the same enemy. In Mississippi an autocratic and powerful minority rules, through organized violence, to suppress the vast, virtually powerless, majority. In California, the privileged minority manipulates the University bureaucracy to suppress the students' political expression. That "respectable" bureaucracy masks the financial plutocrats; that impersonal bureaucracy is the efficient enemy in a "Brave New World."

In our free speech fight at the University of California, we have come up against what may emerge as the greatest problem of our nation—depersonalized, unresponsive bureaucracy. We have encoun-

---

Reprinted in Paul Jacobs and Saul Landau, eds., *The New Radicals: A Report with Documents* (New York: Vintage, 1966), 230–34.

tered the organized status quo in Mississippi, but it is the same in Berkeley. Here we find it impossible usually to meet with anyone but secretaries. Beyond that, we find functionaries who cannot make policy but can only hide behind the rules. We have discovered total lack of response on the part of the policy makers. To grasp a situation which is truly Kafkaesque, it is necessary to understand the bureaucratic mentality. And we have learned quite a bit about it this fall, more outside the classroom than in.

As bureaucrat, an administrator believes that nothing new happens. He occupies an ahistorical point of view. In September, to get the attention of this bureaucracy which had issued arbitrary edicts suppressing student political expression and refused to discuss its action, we held a sit-in on the campus. We sat around a police car and kept it immobilized for over thirty-two hours. At last, the administrative bureaucracy agreed to negotiate. But instead, on the following Monday, we discovered that a committee had been appointed, in accordance with usual regulations, to resolve the dispute. Our attempt to convince any of the administrators that an event had occurred, that something new had happened, failed. They saw this simply as something to be handled by normal university procedures.

The same is true of all bureaucracies. They begin as tools, means to certain legitimate goals, and they end up feeding their own existence. The conception that bureaucrats have is that history has in fact come to an end. No events can occur now that the Second World War is over which can change American society substantially. We proceed by standard procedures as we are.

The most crucial problems facing the United States today are the problem of automation and the problem of racial injustice. Most people who will be put out of jobs by machines will not accept an end to events, this historical plateau, as the point beyond which no change occurs. Negroes will not accept an end to history here. All of us must refuse to accept history's final judgment that in America there is no place in society for people whose skins are dark. On campus, students are not about to accept it as fact that the university has ceased evolving and is in its final state of perfection, that students and faculty are respectively raw material and employees, or that the University is to be autocratically run by unresponsive bureaucrats.

Here is the real contradiction: the bureaucrats hold history as ended. As a result significant parts of the population both on campus and off are dispossessed, and these dispossessed are not about to accept this ahistorical point of view. It is out of this that the conflict has occurred with the university bureaucracy and will continue to occur until that bureaucracy becomes responsive or until it is clear the university cannot function.

The things we are asking for in our civil rights protests have a deceptively quaint ring. We are asking for the due process of law. We are asking for our actions to be judged by committees of our peers. We are asking that regulations ought to be considered as arrived at legitimately only from the consensus of the governed. These phrases are all pretty old, but they are not being taken seriously in America today, nor are they being taken seriously on the Berkeley campus.

I have just come from a meeting with the Dean of Students. She notified us that she was aware of certain violations of university regulations by certain organizations. University friends of SNCC, which I represent, was one of these. We tried to draw from her some statement on these great principles: consent of the governed, jury of one's peers, due process. The best she could do was to evade or to present the administration party line. It is very hard to make any contact with the human being who is behind these organizations.

The university is the place where people begin seriously to question the conditions of their existence and raise the issue of whether they can be committed to the society they have been born into. After a long period of apathy during the fifties, students have begun not only to question but, having arrived at answers, to act on those answers. This is part of a growing understanding among many people in America that history has not ended, that a better society is possible, and that it is worth dying for.

This free speech fight points up a fascinating aspect of contemporary campus life. Students are permitted to talk all they want so long as their speech has no consequences.

One conception of the university, suggested by a classical Christian formulation, is that it be in the world but not of the world. The conception of Clark Kerr [university chancellor], by contrast, is that the university is part and parcel of this particular stage in the history of American society; it stands to serve the need of American industry; it is a factory that turns out a certain product needed by industry or government. Because speech does often have consequences which might alter this perversion of higher education, the university must put itself in a position of censorship. It can permit two kinds of speech: speech which encourages continuation of the status quo, and speech which advocates changes in it so radical as to be irrelevant in the foreseeable future. Someone may advocate radical change in all aspects of

American society, and this I am sure he can do with impunity. But if someone advocates sit-ins to bring about changes in discriminatory hiring practices, this can not be permitted because it goes against the status quo of which the university is a part. And that is how the fight began here.

The administration of the Berkeley campus has admitted that external, extra-legal groups have pressured the university not to permit students on campus to organize picket lines, not to permit on campus any speech with consequences. And the bureaucracy went along. Speech with consequences, speech in the area of civil rights, speech which some might regard as illegal, must stop.

Many students here at the university, many people in society, are wandering aimlessly about. Strangers in their own lives, there is no place for them. They are people who have not learned to compromise, who for example have come to the university to learn to question, to grow, to learn—all the standard things that sound like clichés because no one takes them seriously. And they find at one point or other that for them to become part of society, to become lawyers, ministers, businessmen, people in government, that very often they must compromise those principles which were most dear to them. They must suppress the most creative impulses that they have; this is a prior condition for being part of the system. The university is well structured, well tooled, to turn out people with all the sharp edges worn off, the well-rounded person. The university is well equipped to produce that sort of person, and this means that the best among the people who enter must for four years wander aimlessly much of the time questioning why they are on campus at all, doubting whether there is any point in what they are doing, and looking toward a very bleak existence afterward in a game in which all of the rules have been made up, which one cannot really amend.

It is a bleak scene, but it is all a lot of us have to look forward to. Society provides no challenge. American society in the standard conception it has of itself is simply no longer exciting. The most exciting things going on in America today are movements to change America. America is becoming ever more the utopia of sterilized, automated contentment. The "futures" and "careers" for which American students now prepare are for the most part intellectual and moral wastelands. This chrome-plated consumers' paradise would have us grow up to be well-behaved children. But an important minority of men and women coming to the front today have shown that they will die rather than be standardized, replaceable, and irrelevant.

19

LYNDON B. JOHNSON

The American Promise: Special Message to the Congress
March 15, 1965

Rarely has a president responded so directly to radical protest as in this speech Lyndon B. Johnson gave to Congress on March 15, 1965, just after the bloody repression of protests in Selma, Alabama. LBJ indicted segregation with the authority of a white southerner who had upheld it for decades. In an extraordinary gesture, he invoked the slogan of the civil rights movement by declaring with great firmness, "We shall overcome." Concretely, he demanded a voting rights act that would guarantee African Americans a share of power in the United States, and he got it. The act passed in August 1965, mandating federal elections registrars in any county where 40 percent of the eligible voters were not registered. It was the most direct intervention in state and local politics since Reconstruction.

Mr. Speaker, Mr. President, Members of the Congress:

I speak tonight for the dignity of man and the destiny of democracy.

I urge every member of both parties, Americans of all religions and of all colors, from every section of this country, to join me in that cause.

At times history and fate meet at a single time in a single place to shape a turning point in man's unending search for freedom. So it was at Lexington and Concord. So it was a century ago at Appomattox. So it was last week in Selma, Alabama.

There, long-suffering men and women peacefully protested the denial of their rights as Americans. Many were brutally assaulted. One good man, a man of God, was killed.[1]

[1] The Reverend James Reeb, a white Unitarian minister from the North, had been beaten to death by white thugs in Selma. SNCC activists such as Stokely Carmichael noted acidly that Johnson had failed to mention Jimmy Lee Jackson, a black youth killed when he tried to protect his mother from a beating by a state trooper.

Lyndon B. Johnson, *Public Papers of the Presidents of the United States: Lyndon B. Johnson, 1965* (Washington, D.C.: Government Printing Office, 1965), 1:281–87.

There is no cause for pride in what has happened in Selma. There is no cause for self-satisfaction in the long denial of equal rights of millions of Americans. But there is cause for hope and for faith in our democracy in what is happening here tonight.

For the cries of pain and the hymns and protests of oppressed people have summoned into convocation all the majesty of this great Government—the Government of the greatest Nation on earth.

Our mission is at once the oldest and the most basic of this country: to right wrong, to do justice, to serve man.

In our time we have come to live with moments of great crisis. Our lives have been marked with debate about great issues; issues of war and peace, issues of prosperity and depression. But rarely in any time does an issue lay bare the secret heart of America itself. Rarely are we met with a challenge, not to our growth or abundance, our welfare or our security, but rather to the values and the purposes and the meaning of our beloved Nation.

The issue of equal rights for American Negroes is such an issue. And should we defeat every enemy, should we double our wealth and conquer the stars, and still be unequal to this issue, then we will have failed as a people and as a nation.

For with a country as with a person, "What is a man profited, if he shall gain the whole world, and lose his own soul?"

There is no Negro problem. There is no Southern problem. There is no Northern problem. There is only an American problem. And we are met here tonight as Americans—not as Democrats or Republicans—we are met here as Americans to solve that problem.

This was the first nation in the history of the world to be founded with a purpose. The great phrases of that purpose still sound in every American heart, North and South: "All men are created equal"—"government by consent of the governed"—"give me liberty or give me death." Well, those are not just clever words, or those are not just empty theories. In their name Americans have fought and died for two centuries, and tonight around the world they stand there as guardians of our liberty, risking their lives.

Those words are a promise to every citizen that he shall share in the dignity of man. This dignity cannot be found in a man's possessions; it cannot be found in his power, or in his position. It really rests on his right to be treated as a man equal in opportunity to all others. It says that he shall share in freedom, he shall choose his leaders, educate his children, and provide for his family according to his ability and his merits as a human being.

To apply any other test—to deny a man his hopes because of his color or race, his religion or the place of his birth—is not only to do injustice, it is to deny America and to dishonor the dead who gave their lives for American freedom.

The Right to Vote

Our fathers believed that if this noble view of the rights of man was to flourish, it must be rooted in democracy. The most basic right of all was the right to choose your own leaders. The history of this country, in large measure, is the history of the expansion of that right to all of our people.

Many of the issues of civil rights are very complex and most difficult. But about this there can and should be no argument. Every American citizen must have an equal right to vote. There is no reason which can excuse the denial of that right. There is no duty which weighs more heavily on us than the duty we have to ensure that right.

Yet the harsh fact is that in many places in this country men and women are kept from voting simply because they are Negroes.

Every device of which ingenuity is capable has been used to deny this right. The Negro citizen may go to register only to be told that the day is wrong, or the hour is late, or the official in charge is absent. And if he persists, and if he manages to present himself to the registrar, he may be disqualified because he did not spell out his middle name or because he abbreviated a word on the application.

And if he manages to fill out an application he is given a test. The registrar is the sole judge of whether he passes this test. He may be asked to recite the entire Constitution, or explain the most complex provisions of State law. And even a college degree cannot be used to prove that he can read and write.

For the fact is that the only way to pass these barriers is to show a white skin.

Experience has clearly shown that the existing process of law cannot overcome systematic and ingenious discrimination. No law that we now have on the books—and I have helped to put three of them there—can ensure the right to vote when local officials are determined to deny it.

In such a case our duty must be clear to all of us. The Constitution says that no person shall be kept from voting because of his race or his color. We have all sworn an oath before God to support and to defend that Constitution. We must now act in obedience to that oath.

Guaranteeing the Right to Vote

Wednesday I will send to Congress a law designed to eliminate illegal barriers to the right to vote. . . .

This bill will strike down restrictions to voting in all elections — Federal, State, and local — which have been used to deny Negroes the right to vote.

This bill will establish a simple, uniform standard which cannot be used, however ingenious the effort, to flout our Constitution.

It will provide for citizens to be registered by officials of the United States Government if the State officials refuse to register them.

It will eliminate tedious, unnecessary lawsuits which delay the right to vote.

Finally, this legislation will ensure that properly registered individuals are not prohibited from voting. . . .

The Need for Action

There is no constitutional issue here. The command of the constitution is plain. There is no moral issue. It is wrong — deadly wrong — to deny any of your fellow Americans the right to vote in this country.

There is no issue of States rights or national rights. There is only the struggle for human rights.

I have not the slightest doubt what will be your answer. . . .

We Shall Overcome

But even if we pass this bill, the battle will not be over. What happened in Selma is part of a far larger movement which reaches into every section and State of America. It is the effort of American Negroes to secure for themselves the full blessings of American life.

Their cause must be our cause too. Because it is not just Negroes, but really it is all of us, who must overcome the crippling legacy of bigotry and injustice.

And we shall overcome.

As a man whose roots go deeply into Southern soil I know how agonizing racial feelings are. I know how difficult it is to reshape the attitudes and the structure of our society.

But a century has passed, more than a hundred years, since the Negro was freed. And he is not fully free tonight.

It was more than a hundred years ago that Abraham Lincoln, a great President of another party, signed the Emancipation Proclamation, but emancipation is a proclamation and not a fact.

A century has passed, more than a hundred years, since equality was promised. And yet the Negro is not equal.

A century has passed since the day of promise. And the promise is unkept.

The time of justice has now come. I tell you that I believe sincerely that no force can hold it back. It is right in the eyes of man and God that it should come. And when it does, I think that day will brighten the lives of every American.

For Negroes are not the only victims. How many white children have gone uneducated, how many white families have lived in stark poverty, how many white lives have been scarred by fear, because we have wasted our energy and our substance to maintain the barriers of hatred and terror?

So I say to all of you here, and to all in the Nation tonight, that those who appeal to you to hold on to the past do so at the cost of denying you your future.

This great, rich, restless country can offer opportunity and education and hope to all: black and white, North and South, sharecropper and city dweller. These are the enemies: poverty, ignorance, disease. They are the enemies and not our fellow man, not our neighbor. And these enemies too, poverty, disease and ignorance, we shall overcome. . . .

20

PAUL POTTER

The Incredible War
April 17, 1965

In November 1964, Lyndon Johnson was the "peace candidate," promising "no wider war" in Vietnam. The following year, however, in early 1965, he initiated massive bombing of North Vietnam and sent tens of thousands of ground troops into the conflict. That April, 20,000 Americans

Reprinted in Massimo Teodori, ed., *The New Left: A Documentary History* (Indianapolis: Bobbs-Merrill, 1969), 246–48.

rallied against the war in Washington, D.C., making the antiwar move-
ment a visible influence in national politics. The rally was organized by
SDS, and in his speech to the crowd, SDS president Paul Potter stressed
that the antiwar cause was part of "a movement to build a more decent
society." He also linked Vietnamese peasants fighting for freedom and
national liberation under Communist leadership with campaigns for jus-
tice by poor people in the United States. This marked a new solidarity
across national borders and the cold war divide.

The incredible war in Vietnam has provided the razor, the terrifying
sharp cutting edge that has finally severed the last vestiges of illusion
that morality and democracy are the guiding principles of American
foreign policy. The saccharine, self-righteous moralism that promises
the Vietnamese a billion dollars of economic and social destruction
and political repression is rapidly losing what power it might ever have
had to reassure us about the decency of our foreign policy. . . .

The President says that we are defending freedom in Vietnam.
Whose freedom? Not the freedom of the Vietnamese. The first act
of the first dictator (Diem[1]) the U.S. installed in Vietnam was to sys-
tematically begin the persecution of all political opposition, non-
Communist as well as Communist. . . .

The pattern of repression and destruction that we have developed
and justified in the war is so thorough that it can only be called "cultural genocide." I am not simply talking about napalm or gas or crop
destruction or torture hurled indiscriminately on women and children,
insurgent and neutral, upon the first suspicion of rebel activity. That in
itself is horrendous and incredible beyond belief. But it is only part of
a large pattern of destruction to the very fabric of the country. We
have uprooted the people from the land and imprisoned them in concentration camps called "sunrise villages." Through conscription and
direct political intervention and control we have broken or destroyed
local customs and traditions, trampled upon those things of value
which give dignity and purpose to life. . . .

Not even the President can say that this is war to defend the freedom of the Vietnamese people. Perhaps what the President means
when he speaks of freedom is the freedom of the Americans.

---

[1]Ngo Dinh Diem was an anti-Communist Catholic aristocrat who was president of
South Vietnam from 1954 to October 1963, when he was deposed and killed in a military coup supported by the CIA.

What in fact has the war done for freedom in America? It has led to even more vigorous governmental efforts to control information, manipulate the press and pressure and persuade the public through distorted or downright dishonest documents such as the White Paper on Vietnam.[2] . . .

In many ways this is an unusual march, because the large majority of the people here are not involved in a peace movement as their primary basis of concern. What is exciting about the participants in this march is that so many of us view ourselves consciously as participants as well in a movement to build a more decent society. There are students here who have been involved in protest over the quality and kind of education they are receiving in growingly bureaucratized, depersonalized institutions called universities; there are Negroes from Mississippi and Alabama who are struggling against the tyranny and repression of those states; there are poor people here—Negro and white—from Northern urban areas who are attempting to build movements that abolish poverty and secure democracy; there are faculty who are beginning to question the relevance of their institutions to the critical problems facing the society. . . .

Thus far the war in Vietnam has only dramatized the demand of ordinary people to have some opportunity to make their own lives, and of their unwillingness, even under incredible odds, to give up the struggle against external domination. We are told however that that struggle can be legitimately suppressed since it might lead to the development of a Communist system—and before that menace, all criticism is supposed to melt.

This is a critical point and there are several things that must be said here—not by way of celebration, but because I think they are the truth. First, if this country were serious about giving the people of Vietnam some alternative to a Communist social revolution, that opportunity was sacrificed in 1954 when we helped to install Diem and his repression of non-Communist movements. There is no indication that we were serious about that goal—that we were ever willing to contemplate the risks of allowing the Vietnamese to choose their own destinies. Second, those people who insist now that Vietnam can be neutralized are for the most part looking for a sugar coating to cover the bitter pill. We must accept the consequences that calling for an

---

[2]In 1965, the State Department released an authoritative white paper asserting that North Vietnam was the cause of the civil war in Vietnam and that the United States was simply aiding a democratic ally.

end of the war in Vietnam is in fact allowing for the likelihood that a Vietnam without war will be a self-styled Communist Vietnam. Third, this country must come to understand that the creation of a Communist country in the world today is not an ultimate defeat. If people are given the opportunity to choose their own lives it is likely that some of them will choose what we have called "Communist systems." . . .

But the war goes on; the freedom to conduct that war depends on the dehumanization not only of Vietnamese people but of Americans as well; it depends on the construction of a system of premises and thinking that insulates the President and his advisers thoroughly and completely from the human consequences of the decisions they make. I do not believe that the President or Mr. Rusk [secretary of state] or Mr. McNamara [secretary of defense] or even McGeorge Bundy [national security adviser] are particularly evil men. If asked to throw napalm on the back of a 10-year-old child they would shrink in horror—but their decisions have led to mutilation and death of thousands and thousands of people.

What kind of system is it that allows "good" men to make those kinds of decisions? What kind of system is it that justifies the U.S. or any country seizing the destinies of the Vietnamese people and using them callously for our own purpose? What kind of system is it that disenfranchises people in the South, leaves millions upon millions of people throughout the country impoverished and excluded from the mainstream and promise of American society, that creates faceless and terrible bureaucracies and makes those the place where people spend their lives and do their work, that consistently puts material values before human values—and still persists in calling itself free and still persists in finding itself fit to police the world? . . .

We must name that system. We must name it, describe it, analyze it, understand it and change it. For it is only when that system is changed and brought under control that there can be any hope for stopping the forces that create a war in Vietnam today or a murder in the South tomorrow. . . .

If the people of this country are to end the war in Vietnam, and to change the institutions which create it, then, the people of this country must create a massive social movement—and if that can be built around the issue of Vietnam, then that is what we must do. . . .

But that means that we build a movement that works not simply in Washington but in communities and with the problems that face people throughout the society. That means that we build a movement that understands Vietnam, in all its horror, as but a symptom of a deeper malaise, that we build a movement that makes possible the implementation of the values that would have prevented Vietnam, a movement based on the integrity of man and a belief in man's capacity to determine his own life; a movement that does not exclude people because they are too poor or have been held down; a movement that has the capacity to tolerate all of the formulations of society that men may choose to strive for; a movement that will build on the new and creative forms of protest that are beginning to emerge, such as the teach-in, and extend their efforts and intensify them; a movement that will not tolerate the escalation or prolongation of this war but will, if necessary, respond to the Administration war effort with massive civil disobedience all over the country that will wrench the country into a confrontation with the issues of the war; a movement that must of necessity reach out to all those people in Vietnam or elsewhere who are struggling to find decency and control for their lives.

For in a strange way the people of Vietnam and the people on this demonstration are united in much more than a common concern that the war be ended. In both countries there are people struggling to build a movement that has the power to change their condition. The system that frustrates these movements is the same. All our lives, our destinies, our very hopes to live depend on our ability to overcome that system. . . .

21

CASEY HAYDEN AND MARY KING

Sex and Caste

November 18, 1965

In 1964–65, some young white women in SNCC began to examine their roles. Why did they do all the "shit work" and not share in the decision making or public speaking? Based on months of informal conversations, the respected movement veterans Mary King and Casey Hayden circulated

Reprinted in Sara Evans, *Personal Politics: The Origins of Women's Liberation in the Civil Rights Movement and the New Left* (New York: Vintage, 1979), 235–38.

this memo to young women around the country. Their goal was simply to start a dialogue about women's exclusion from structures of power and their subordination in personal relationships. Although King and Hayden thought that "the chances seem nil that we could start a movement based on anything as distant to general American thought as a sex-caste system," that is exactly what happened. The memo noted that male radicals' usual response to discussions of women's oppression was laughter. This pattern of derision, repeated over several years, eventually led many of these women to leave male-dominated organizations.

A kind of memo from Casey Hayden and Mary King to a number of other women in the peace and freedom movements.

We've talked a lot to each other and to some of you, about our own and other women's problems in trying to live in our personal lives and in our work as independent and creative people. In these conversations we've found what seem to be recurrent ideas or themes. Maybe we can look at these things many of us perceive, often as a result of insights learned from the movements:

Sex and Caste

There seem to be many parallels that can be drawn between treatment of Negroes and treatment of women in our society as a whole. But in particular, women we've talked to who work in the movement seem to be caught up in a common-law caste system that operates, sometimes subtly, forcing them to work around or outside hierarchical structures of power which may exclude them. Women seem to be placed in the same position of assumed subordination in personal situations too. It is a caste system which, at its worst, uses and exploits women.

This is complicated by several facts, among them: (1) The caste system is not institutionalized by law (women have the right to vote, to sue for divorce, etc.); (2) Women can't withdraw from the situation (a la nationalism) or overthrow it; (3) There are biological differences (even though those biological differences are usually discussed or accepted without taking present and future technology into account so we probably can't be sure what these differences mean). Many people who are very hip to the implications of the racial caste system, even people in the movement, don't seem to be able to see the sexual caste system and if the question is raised they respond with: "That's the way it's supposed to be. There are biological differences." Or with other statements which recall a white segregationist confronted with integration.

Women and Problems of Work

The caste system perspective dictates the roles assigned to women in the movement, and certainly even more to women outside the movement. Within the movement, questions arise in situations ranging from relationships of women organizers to men in the community, to who cleans the freedom house, to who holds leadership positions, to who does secretarial work, and who acts as spokesman for groups. Other problems arise between women with varying degrees of awareness of themselves as being as capable as men but held back from full participation, or between women who see themselves as needing more control of their work than other women demand. And there are problems with relationships between white women and black women.

Women and Personal Relations with Men

Having learned from the movement to think radically about the personal worth and abilities of people whose role in society had gone unchallenged before, a lot of women in the movement have begun trying to apply those lessons to their own relations with men. Each of us probably has her own story of the various results, and of the internal struggle occasioned by trying to break out of very deeply learned fears, needs, and self-perceptions, and of what happens when we try to replace them with concepts of people and freedom learned from the movement and organizing.

Institutions

Nearly everyone has real questions about those institutions which shape perspectives on men and women: marriage, child rearing patterns, women's (and men's) magazines, etc. People are beginning to think about and even to experiment with new forms in these areas.

Men's Reactions to the Questions Raised Here

A very few men seem to feel, when they hear conversations involving these problems, that they have a right to be present and participate in them, since they are so deeply involved. At the same time, very few men can respond non-defensively, since the whole idea is either beyond their comprehension or threatens and exposes them. The usual response is laughter. That inability to see the whole issue as serious, as the strait-jacketing of both sexes, and as societally determined often shapes our own response so that we learn to think in their terms about ourselves and to feel silly rather than trust our inner feelings. The problems we're listing here, and what others have said about them, are therefore largely drawn from conversations among women only—and that difficulty in establishing dialogue with men is a recurring theme among people we've talked to.

Lack of Community for Discussion

Nobody is writing, or organizing or talking publicly about women, in any way that reflects the problems that various women in the movement come across and which we've tried to touch above. Consider this quote from an article in the centennial issue of *The Nation:*

> However equally we consider men and women, the work plans for husbands and wives cannot be given equal weight. A woman should not aim for "a second-level career" because she is a *woman;* from girlhood on she should recognize that, if she is also going to be a wife and mother, she will not be able to give as much to her work as she would if single. That is, she should not feel that she cannot aspire to directing the laboratory simply because she is a woman, but rather because she is also a wife and mother; as such, her work as a lab technician (or the equivalent in another field) should bring both satisfaction and the knowledge that, through it, she is fulfilling an additional role, making an additional contribution.

And that's about as deep as the analysis goes publicly, which is not nearly so deep as we've heard many of you go in chance conversations.

The reason we want to try to open up dialogue is mostly subjective. Working in the movement often intensifies personal problems, especially if we start trying to apply things we're learning there to our personal lives. Perhaps we can start to talk with each other more openly than in the past and create a community of support for each other so we can deal with ourselves and others with integrity and can therefore keep working.

Objectively, the chances seem nil that we could start a movement based on anything as distant to general American thought as a sex-caste system. Therefore, most of us will probably want to work full time on problems such as war, poverty, race. The very fact that the country can't face, much less deal with, the questions we're raising means that the movement is one place to look for some relief. Real efforts at dialogue within the movement and with whatever liberal groups, community women, or students might listen are justified. That is, all the problems between men and women and all the problems of women functioning in society as equal human beings are among the most basic that people face. We've talked in the movement about trying to build a society which would see basic human problems (which are now seen as private troubles), as public problems and would try to shape institutions to meet human needs rather than shaping people to meet the needs of those with power. To raise questions like those above illustrates very directly that society hasn't dealt with some of its deepest problems and opens discussion of why that is so. (In one sense, it is a radicalizing question that can take people beyond legalistic solutions into areas of personal and institutional change.) The second objective reason we'd like to see discussion begin is that we've learned a great deal in the movement and perhaps this is one area where a determined attempt to apply ideas we've learned there can produce some new alternatives.

22

BLACK PANTHER PARTY FOR SELF-DEFENSE

The Ten-Point Program:
What We Want/What We Believe
October 1966

Black Panther Party founders Huey P. Newton and Bobby Seale had drifted in and out of black nationalist groups, and Newton had read voraciously in philosophy and third world politics. In late 1966, they acquired weapons and uniforms (leather jackets and black berets), and

Reprinted in Philip S. Foner, ed., *The Black Panthers Speak: The Manifesto of the Party: The First Complete Documentary Record of the Panthers' Program* (Philadelphia: J. B. Lippincott, 1970), 2–4.

Newton issued the party's Ten-Point Program. This platform embodied the complexity of the Black Power movement, demanding both practical reforms such as guaranteed jobs and housing and a United Nations–organized referendum "to be held throughout the black colony . . . for the purpose of determining the will of black people as to their national destiny." A measure of Newton's intellectual audacity can be seen in point 10, where he claimed America's revolutionary legacy as his own.

---

1. *We want freedom. We want power to determine the destiny of our Black Community.*

We believe that black people will not be free until we are able to determine our destiny.

2. *We want full employment for our people.*

We believe that the federal government is responsible and obligated to give every man employment or a guaranteed income. We believe that if the white American businessmen will not give full employment, then the means of production should be taken from the businessmen and placed in the community so that the people of the community can organize and employ all of its people and give a high standard of living.

3. *We want an end to the robbery by the white man of our Black Community.*

We believe that this racist government has robbed us and now we are demanding the overdue debt of forty acres and two mules. Forty acres and two mules was promised 100 years ago as restitution for slave labor and mass murder of black people. We will accept the payment in currency which will be distributed to our many communities. The Germans are now aiding the Jews in Israel for the genocide of the Jewish people. The Germans murdered six million Jews. The American racist has taken part in the slaughter of over fifty million black people; therefore, we feel that this is a modest demand that we make.

4. *We want decent housing, fit for shelter of human beings.*

We believe that if the white landlords will not give decent housing to our black community, then the housing and the land should be made into cooperatives so that our community, with government aid, can build and make decent housing for its people.

5. *We want education for our people that exposes the true nature of this decadent American society. We want education that teaches us our true history and our role in the present-day society.*

We believe in an educational system that will give to our people a knowledge of self. If a man does not have knowledge of himself and his position in society and the world, then he has little chance to relate to anything else.

6. *We want all black men to be exempt from military service.*

We believe that Black people should not be forced to fight in the military service to defend a racist government that does not protect us. We will not fight and kill other people of color in the world who, like black people, are being victimized by the white racist government of America. We will protect ourselves from the force and violence of the racist police and the racist military, by whatever means necessary.

7. *We want an immediate end to POLICE BRUTALITY and MURDER of black people.*

We believe we can end police brutality in our black community by organizing black self-defense groups that are dedicated to defending our black community from racist police oppression and brutality. The Second Amendment to the Constitution of the United States gives a right to bear arms. We therefore believe that all black people should arm themselves for self-defense.

8. *We want freedom for all black men held in federal, state, county and city prisons and jails.*

We believe that all black people should be released from the many jails and prisons because they have not received a fair and impartial trial.

9. *We want all black people when brought to trial to be tried in court by a jury of their peer group or people from their black communities, as defined by the Constitution of the United States.*

We believe that the courts should follow the United States Constitution so that black people will receive fair trials. The 14th Amendment of the U.S. Constitution gives a man a right to be tried by his peer group. A peer is a person from a similar economic, social, religious, geographical, environmental, historical and racial background. To do this the court will be forced to select a jury from the black community from which the black defendant came. We have been, and are being tried by all-white juries that have no understanding of the "average reasoning man" of the black community.

10. *We want land, bread, housing, education, clothing, justice and peace. And as our major political objective, a United Nations–supervised plebiscite to be held throughout the black colony in which only black colonial subjects will be allowed to participate, for the purpose of determining the will of black people as to their national destiny.*

When, in the course of human events, it becomes necessary for one people to dissolve the political bands which have connected them with another, and to assume, among the powers of the earth, the separate and equal station to which the laws of nature and nature's God entitle them, a decent respect to the opinions of mankind requires that they should declare the causes which impel them to the separation.

We hold these truths to be self-evident, that all men are created equal; that they are endowed by their Creator with certain unalienable rights; that among these are life, liberty, and the pursuit of happiness. *That, to secure these rights, governments are instituted among men, deriving their just powers from the consent of the governed; that, whenever any form of government becomes destructive of these ends, it is the right of the people to alter or to abolish it, and to institute a new government, laying its foundation on such principles, and organizing its powers in such form, as to them shall seem most likely to effect their safety and happiness.* Prudence, indeed, will dictate that governments long established should not be changed for light and transient causes; and, accordingly, all experience hath shown, that mankind are more disposed to suffer, while evils are sufferable, than to right themselves by abolishing the forms to which they are accustomed. *But, when a long train of abuses and usurpations, pursuing invariably the same object, evinces a design to reduce them under absolute despotism, it is their right, it is their duty, to throw off such government, and to provide new guards for their future security.*

23

NATIONAL ORGANIZATION FOR WOMEN

Statement of Purpose

October 29, 1966

In 1966, female professionals, civil servants, trade unionists, and academics formed the National Organization for Women (NOW) as a civil rights organization that would campaign, lobby, and protest on women's behalf. As its Statement of Purpose makes clear, NOW's original priority was the public sphere of jobs and educational discrimination. The urgency of its mission was underscored by the fact that women had not held their own in the past generation, instead losing ground in pay, employment status, and representation in politics, the professions, and higher education. Eventually, NOW also took up the "personal politics" of sexuality, reproduction, and male violence against women.

We, men and women who hereby constitute ourselves as the National Organization for Women, believe that the time has come for a new movement toward true equality for all women in America, and toward a fully equal partnership of the sexes, as part of the world-wide revolution of human rights now taking place within and beyond our national borders.

The purpose of NOW is to take action to bring women into full participation in the mainstream of American society now, exercising all the privileges and responsibilities thereof in truly equal partnership with men.

We believe the time has come to move beyond the abstract argument, discussion, and symposia over the status and special nature of women which has raged in America in recent years; the time has come to confront, with concrete action, the conditions that now prevent women from enjoying the equality of opportunity and freedom of

Reprinted in Miriam Schneir, ed., *Feminism in Our Time: The Essential Writings, World War II to the Present* (New York: Vintage, 1994), 96–102.

choice which is their right, as individual Americans, and as human beings.

NOW is dedicated to the proposition that women, first and foremost, are human beings, who, like all other people in our society, must have the chance to develop their fullest human potential. We believe that women can achieve such equality only by accepting to the full the challenges and responsibilities they share with all other people in our society, as part of the decision-making mainstream of American political, economic, and social life.

We organize to initiate or support action, nationally, or in any part of this nation, by individuals or organizations, to break through the silken curtain of prejudice and discrimination against women in government, industry, the professions, the churches, the political parties, the judiciary, the labor unions, in education, science, medicine, law, religion, and every other field of importance in American society.

Enormous changes taking place in our society make it both possible and urgently necessary to advance the unfinished revolution of women toward true equality, now. With a life span lengthened to nearly seventy-five years it is no longer either necessary or possible for women to devote the greater part of their lives to child-rearing; yet childbearing and rearing—which continues to be a most important part of most women's lives—still is used to justify barring women from equal professional and economic participation and advance.

Today's technology has reduced most of the productive chores which women once performed in the home and in mass-production industries based upon routine unskilled labor. This same technology has virtually eliminated the quality of muscular strength as a criterion for filling most jobs, while intensifying American industry's need for creative intelligence. In view of this new industrial revolution created by automation in the mid-twentieth century, women can and must participate in old and new fields of society in full equality—or become permanent outsiders.

Despite all the talk about the status of American women in recent years, the actual position of women in the United States has declined, and is declining, to an alarming degree throughout the 1950s and '60s. Although 46.4 percent of all American women between the ages of eighteen and sixty-five now work outside the home, the overwhelming majority—75 percent—are in routine clerical, sales, or factory jobs, or they are household workers, cleaning women, hospital attendants. About two-thirds of Negro women workers are in the lowest paid service occupations. Working women are becoming increasingly—not less—concentrated on the bottom of the job ladder. As a consequence full-time women workers today earn on the average only 60 percent of what men earn, and that wage gap has been increasing over the past twenty-five years in every major industry group. . . .

Further, with higher education increasingly essential in today's society, too few women are entering and finishing college or going on to graduate or professional school. Today, women earn only one in three of the B.A.'s and M.A.'s granted, and one in ten of the Ph.D.'s.

In all the professions considered of importance to society, and in the executive ranks of industry and government, women are losing ground. Where they are present it is only a token handful. Women comprise less than 1 percent of federal judges; less than 4 percent of all lawyers; 7 percent of doctors. Yet women represent 51 percent of the U.S. population. And, increasingly, men are replacing women in the top positions in secondary and elementary schools, in social work, and in libraries—once thought to be women's fields.

Official pronouncements of the advance in the status of women hide not only the reality of this dangerous decline, but the fact that nothing is being done to stop [it]. The excellent reports of the President's Commission on the Status of Women and of the state commissions have not been fully implemented. Such commissions have power only to advise. They have no power to enforce their recommendations; nor have they the freedom to organize American women and men to press for action on them. The reports of these commissions have, however, created a basis upon which it is now possible to build.

Discrimination in employment on the basis of sex is now prohibited by federal law, in Title VII of the Civil Rights Act of 1964. But although nearly one-third of the cases brought before the Equal Employment Opportunity Commission during the first year dealt with sex discrimination and the proportion is increasing dramatically, the Commission has not made clear its intention to enforce the law with the same seriousness on behalf of women as of other victims of discrimination. Many of these cases were Negro women, who are the victims of the double discrimination of race and sex. Until now, too few women's organizations and official spokesmen have been willing to speak out against these dangers facing women. Too many women have been restrained by the fear of being called "feminist."

There is no civil rights movement to speak for women, as there has been for Negroes and other victims of discrimination. The National Organization for Women must therefore begin to speak. . . .

24

STOKELY CARMICHAEL
AND CHARLES V. HAMILTON

Black Power

1967

From 1966 to 1968, Stokely Carmichael was the public face of Black Power, as SNCC's chairman and a scalding orator of international repute. In 1964–65, he had been a SNCC field secretary in Lowndes County, Alabama, an overwhelmingly black county where not a single black person could vote. He helped build an all-black political party, the Lowndes County Freedom Organization, which pioneered the imagery of the Black Panther. This excerpt from his 1967 book with political scientist Charles V. Hamilton presented a surprisingly moderate argument. Carmichael and Hamilton insisted that blacks had the same right to vote in a bloc and demand representation as white immigrant groups such as the Irish, Jews, and Italians. This demand was denounced as a racist call for "black supremacy" by many, even some civil rights leaders.

... The adoption of the concept of Black Power is one of the most legitimate and healthy developments in American politics and race relations in our time. The concept of Black Power speaks to all the needs mentioned in this chapter. It is a call for black people in this country to unite, to recognize their heritage, to build a sense of community. It is a call for black people to begin to define their own goals, to lead their own organizations and to support those organizations. It is a call to reject the racist institutions and values of this society.

The concept of Black Power rests on a fundamental premise: *Before a group can enter the open society, it must first close ranks.* By this we mean that group solidarity is necessary before a group can operate effectively from a bargaining position of strength in a pluralistic society. Traditionally, each new ethnic group in this society has found the route to social and political viability through the organization of its

Stokely Carmichael and Charles V. Hamilton, *Black Power: The Politics of Liberation in America* (New York: Vintage, 1967), 44–45.

own institutions with which to represent its needs within the larger society. Studies in voting behavior specifically, and political behavior generally, have made it clear that politically the American pot has not melted. Italians vote for Rubino over O'Brien; Irish for Murphy over Goldberg, etc. This phenomenon may seem distasteful to some, but it has been and remains today a central fact of the American political system. . . .

25

MAULANA KARENGA

Nguzo Saba: The Seven Principles
1967

Maulana Karenga, born Ron Everett, was the charismatic founder of an ideology he called "cultural nationalism," which emphasized the unity of all African people and an Afrocentric worldview. In 1965, he created the US organization in Los Angeles, organized around Kawaida *(Swahili for "tradition and reason"). For Karenga, learning African languages, adopting African clothing, and replacing holidays such as Christmas with African-style celebrations such as Kwanzaa were key to Black Power.* Kawaida *was broken down into seven key principles, the* Nguzo Saba, *which emphasized unity and community rather than political organizing and protest. Karenga's cultural nationalism had many supporters and is still influential. Revolutionary nationalists such as the Black Panthers scorned his apolitical Africanism.*

Umoja (Unity)
To strive for and maintain unity in the family, community, nation and race.

Kujichagulia (Self-Determination)
To define ourselves, name ourselves, create for ourselves and speak for ourselves.

www.officialkwanzaawebsite.org/NguzoSaba.html.

Ujima (Collective Work and Responsibility)
To build and maintain our community together and make our brother's and sister's problems our problems and to solve them together.

Ujamaa (Cooperative Economics)
To build and maintain our own stores, shops and other businesses and to profit from them together.

Nia (Purpose)
To make our collective vocation the building and developing of our community in order to restore our people to their traditional greatness.

Kuumba (Creativity)
To do always as much as we can, in the way we can, in order to leave our community more beautiful and beneficial than we inherited it.

Imani (Faith)
To believe with all our heart in our people, our parents, our teachers, our leaders and the righteousness and victory of our struggle.

26

THE RESISTANCE

We Refuse — October 16

1967

From 1947 to 1970, the Selective Service System registered men between the ages of eighteen and twenty-six for compulsory military service; college students received an automatic deferment. A draft card proved that one had registered, so burning one's card was a serious act of civil disobedience. Opposition to the draft was key to the antiwar movement. In cities, towns, and suburbs, draft counseling centers operated from churches. As sons approached their eighteenth birthdays, parents grappled

Reprinted in Marvin E. Gettleman, Jane Franklin, Marilyn B. Young, and H. Bruce Franklin, eds., *Vietnam and America: A Documented History,* 2nd ed. (New York: Grove Press, 1995), 307.

with their feelings about the war. The appearance in 1966 of the Resistance, several hundred organizers working openly and underground to wreck the draft, was a watershed event. These organizers urged young men to burn or turn in their draft cards, refuse induction, and choose prison rather than fleeing the country or seeking a college deferment. This statement, released in April 1967, called for a "mass" turn-in of draft cards on October 16 as part of the planned march on the Pentagon.

The Resistance is a group of men who are bound together by one single and clear commitment: on October 16 we will hand in our draft cards and refuse any further cooperation with the Selective Service System. By doing so we will actively challenge the government's right to draft American men for its criminal war against the people of Vietnam. We of the Resistance feel that we can no longer passively acquiesce to the Selective Service System by accepting its deferments. The American military system depends upon students, those opposed to war, and those with anti–Vietnam war politics wrangling for the respective deferments. Those opposed to the war are dealt with quietly, individually and on the government's terms. If they do not get the deferments, they must individually find some extra-legal alternative. A popular last resort is Canada, and those who go to Canada must be politically silent in order to stay there. Legal draft alternatives are kept within reach of elite groups—good students, those who are able to express objection to all war on religious grounds, and those with the money to hire good lawyers. For the majority of American guys the only alternatives are jail or the army. While those who are most opposed to the war have been silenced, the system that provides the personnel for war crimes continues to function smoothly.

Many who wish to avoid the draft will, of course, choose to accept deferments; many, however, wish to do more than avoid the draft. Resistance means that if the government is to continue its crimes against humanity, it must first deal with our opposition. We do not seek jail, but we do this because as individuals we know of no justifiable alternative and we believe that in time many other American men will also choose to resist the crimes done in their names.

27

MARTIN LUTHER KING JR.

Declaration of Independence from the War in Vietnam

April 4, 1967

Under pressure to preserve the civil rights movement's links to the Johnson administration, King had avoided forceful denunciations of the war. This speech on April 4, 1967, at Riverside Church in New York City, was a final break with cold war liberalism. Going beyond the war, he indicted his own country as "the greatest purveyor of violence in the world today" and insisted that the United States must "get on the right side of the world revolution." Scholars see the speech as part of a deepening commitment to nonviolent revolution. More than any other leader of the left, King had the ability to connect justice and peace, racism and militarism. Though denounced by moderate African American leaders, King was an urgent voice for peace until his assassination exactly one year later.

Over the past two years, as I have moved to break the betrayal of my own silences and to speak from the burnings of my own heart, as I have called for radical departures from the destruction of Vietnam, many persons have questioned me about the wisdom of my path. At the heart of their concerns this query has often loomed large and loud: Why are *you* speaking about the war, Dr. King? Why are *you* joining the voices of dissent? Peace and civil rights don't mix, they say. Aren't you hurting the cause of your people, they ask. And when I hear them, though I often understand the source of their concern, I am nevertheless greatly saddened, for such questions mean that the inquirers have not really known me, my commitment or my calling. Indeed, their questions suggest that they do not know the world in which they live.

In the light of such tragic misunderstanding, I deem it of signal

Reprinted in Marvin E. Gettleman, Jane Franklin, Marilyn B. Young, and H. Bruce Franklin, eds., *Vietnam and America: A Documented History,* 2nd ed. (New York: Grove Press, 1995), 310–18.

importance to try to state clearly why I believe that the path from Dexter Avenue Baptist Church—the church in Montgomery, Alabama, where I began my pastorage—leads clearly to this sanctuary tonight.

I come to this platform to make a passionate plea to my beloved nation. This speech is not addressed to Hanoi or to the National Liberation Front [NLF].[1] It is not addressed to China or to Russia.

Nor is it an attempt to overlook the ambiguity of the total situation and the need for a collective solution to the tragedy of Vietnam. Neither is it an attempt to make North Vietnam or the National Liberation Front paragons of virtue, nor to overlook the role they can play in a successful resolution of the problem. While they both may have justifiable reasons to be suspicious of the good faith of the United States, life and history give eloquent testimony to the fact that conflicts are never resolved without trustful give and take on both sides.

Tonight, however, I wish not to speak with Hanoi and the NLF, but rather to my fellow Americans who, with me, bear the greatest responsibility in ending a conflict that has exacted a heavy price on both continents.

Since I am a preacher by trade, I suppose it is not surprising that I have seven major reasons for bringing Vietnam into the field of my moral vision. There is at the outset a very obvious and almost facile connection between the war in Vietnam and the struggle I, and others, have been waging in America. A few years ago there was a shining moment in that struggle. It seemed as if there was a real promise of hope for the poor—both black and white—through the Poverty Program.[2] Then came the build-up in Vietnam, and I watched the program broken and eviscerated as if it were some idle political plaything of a society gone mad on war, and I knew that America would never invest the necessary funds or energies in rehabilitation of its poor so long as Vietnam continued to draw men and skills and money like some demonic, destructive suction tube. So I was increasingly compelled to see the war as an enemy of the poor and to attack it as such.

Perhaps the more tragic recognition of reality took place when it became clear to me that the war was doing far more than devastating the hopes of the poor at home. It was sending their sons and their brothers and their husbands to fight and to die in extraordinarily high

[1]The National Liberation Front (NLF) was the coalition led by Communists in South Vietnam that was attempting to overthrow the U.S.-backed regime there. Members of this group were commonly known as Vietcong.
[2]By Poverty Program, King means Johnson's War on Poverty, announced with great fanfare in 1964.

proportions relative to the rest of the population. We were taking the young black men who had been crippled by our society and sending them 8000 miles away to guarantee liberties in Southeast Asia which they had not found in Southwest Georgia and East Harlem. So we have been repeatedly faced with the cruel irony of watching Negro and white boys on TV screens as they kill and die together for a nation that has been unable to seat them together in the same schools. So we watch them in brutal solidarity burning the huts of a poor village, but we realize that they would never live on the same block in Detroit. I could not be silent in the face of such cruel manipulation of the poor.

My third reason grows out of my experience in the ghettos of the North over the last three years—especially the last three summers. As I have walked among the desperate, rejected and angry young men, I have told them that Molotov cocktails and rifles would not solve their problems. I have tried to offer them my deepest compassion while maintaining my conviction that social change comes most meaningfully through non-violent action. But, they asked, what about Vietnam? They asked if our own nation wasn't using massive doses of violence to solve its problems, to bring about the changes it wanted. Their questions hit home, and I knew that I could never again raise my voice against the violence of the oppressed in the ghettos without having first spoken clearly to the greatest purveyor of violence in the world today—my own government.

For those who ask the question, "Aren't you a Civil Rights leader?" and thereby mean to exclude me from the movement for peace, I have this further answer. In 1957 when a group of us formed the Southern Christian Leadership Conference, we chose as our motto: "To save the soul of America." We were convinced that we could not limit our vision to certain rights for black people, but instead affirmed the conviction that America would never be free or saved from itself unless the descendants of its slaves were loosed from the shackles they still wear.

Now, it should be incandescently clear that no one who has any concern for the integrity and life of America today can ignore the present war. If America's soul becomes totally poisoned, part of the autopsy must read "Vietnam." It can never be saved so long as it destroys the deepest hopes of men the world over. . . .

If we continue, there will be no doubt in my mind and in the mind of the world that we have no honorable intentions in Vietnam. It will become clear that our minimal expectation is to occupy it as an American colony, and men will not refrain from thinking that our maximum hope is to goad China into a war so that we may bomb her nuclear installations.

The world now demands a maturity of America that we may not be able to achieve. It demands that we admit that we have been wrong from the beginning of our adventure in Vietnam, that we have been detrimental to the life of her people.

In order to atone for our sins and errors in Vietnam, we should take the initiative in bringing the war to a halt. I would like to suggest five concrete things that our government should do immediately to begin the long and difficult process of extricating ourselves from this nightmare:

1. End all bombing in North and South Vietnam.
2. Declare a unilateral cease-fire in the hope that such action will create the atmosphere for negotiation.
3. Take immediate steps to prevent other battlegrounds in Southeast Asia by curtailing our military build-up in Thailand and our interference in Laos.
4. Realistically accept the fact that the National Liberation Front has substantial support in South Vietnam and must thereby play a role in any meaningful negotiations and in any future Vietnam government.
5. Set a date on which we will remove all foreign troops from Vietnam in accordance with the 1954 Geneva Agreement. . . .

Meanwhile, we in the churches and synagogues have a continuing task while we urge our government to disengage itself from a disgraceful commitment. We must be prepared to match actions with words by seeking out every creative means of protest possible.

As we counsel young men concerning military service we must clarify for them our nation's role in Vietnam and challenge them with the alternative of conscientious objection. I am pleased to say that this is the path now being chosen by more than 70 students at my own Alma Mater, Morehouse College, and I recommend it to all who find the American course in Vietnam a dishonorable and unjust one. Moreover, I would encourage all ministers of draft age to give up their ministerial exemptions and seek status as conscientious objectors. Every man of humane convictions must decide on the protest that best suits his convictions, but we must *all* protest.

There is something seductively tempting about stopping there and sending us all off on what in some circles has become a popular crusade against the war in Vietnam. I say we must enter that struggle, but I wish to go on now to say something even more disturbing. The war in Vietnam is but a symptom of a far deeper malady within the American spirit, and if we ignore this sobering reality we will find ourselves organizing clergy- and laymen-concerned committees for the next generation. We will be marching and attending rallies without end unless there is a significant and profound change in American life and policy.

In 1957 a sensitive American official overseas said that it seemed to him that our nation was on the wrong side of a world revolution. During the past ten years we have seen emerge a pattern of suppression which now has justified the presence of U.S. military "advisors" in Venezuela. The need to maintain social stability for our investments accounts for the counterrevolutionary action of American forces in Guatemala. It tells why American helicopters are being used against guerrillas in Colombia and why American napalm and green beret forces have already been active against rebels in Peru. With such activity in mind, the words of John F. Kennedy come back to haunt us. Five years ago he said, "Those who make peaceful revolution impossible will make violent revolution inevitable."

Increasingly, by choice or by accident, this is the role our nation has taken—by refusing to give up the privileges and the pleasures that come from the immense profits of overseas investment.

I am convinced that if we are to get on the right side of the world revolution, we as a nation must undergo a radical revolution of values. When machines and computers, profit and property rights are considered more important than people, the giant triplets of racism, materialism, and militarism are incapable of being conquered.

A true revolution of values will soon cause us to question the fairness and justice of many of our past and present policies. True compassion is more than flinging a coin to a beggar; it is not haphazard and superficial. It comes to see that an edifice which produces beggars needs re-structuring. A true revolution of values will soon look easily on the glaring contrast of poverty and wealth. With righteous indignation, it will look across the seas and see individual capitalists of the West investing huge sums of money in Asia, Africa and South America, only to take the profits out with no concern for the social betterment of the countries, and say: "This is not just." It will look at our alliance with the landed gentry of Latin America and say: "This is not just." The Western arrogance of feeling that it has everything to teach others and nothing to learn from them is not just. A true revolution of values will lay hands on the world order and say of war: "This way of settling differences is not just." This business of burning human beings with napalm, of filling our nation's homes with orphans and widows, of injecting poisonous drugs of hate into the veins of peoples normally humane, of sending men home from dark and bloody battlefields physically handicapped and psychologically deranged, cannot be reconciled with wisdom, justice, and love. A nation that continues year after year to spend more money on military defense than on programs of social uplift is approaching spiritual death.

America, the richest and most powerful nation in the world, can well lead the way in this revolution of values. There is nothing, except a tragic death wish, to prevent us from re-ordering our priorities, so that the pursuit of peace will take precedence over the pursuit of war. There is nothing to keep us from molding a recalcitrant status quo until we have fashioned it into a brotherhood. . . .

These are revolutionary times. All over the globe men are revolting against old systems of exploitation and oppression, and out of the wombs of a frail world, new systems of justice and equality are being born. The shirtless and barefoot people of the land are rising up as never before. "The people who sat in darkness have seen a great light." We in the West must support these revolutions. It is a sad fact that, because of comfort, complacency, a morbid fear of communism, and our proneness to adjust to injustice, the Western nations that initiated so much of the revolutionary spirit of the modern world have now become the arch antirevolutionaries. This has driven many to feel that only Marxism has the revolutionary spirit. Therefore, communism is a judgment against our failure to make democracy real and follow through on the revolutions that we initiated. Our only hope today lies in our ability to recapture the revolutionary spirit and go out into a sometimes hostile world declaring eternal hostility to poverty, racism, and militarism. . . .

28

DANIEL BERRIGAN

Night Flight to Hanoi
1968

Daniel Berrigan was a Jesuit priest, a respected poet, and a pacifist. In 1965, his superiors exiled him to Latin America because of his radical views. On his return, he joined historian Howard Zinn on a mission to accompany U.S. prisoners of war home after being released by the North Vietnamese. This excerpt from his book Night Flight to Hanoi *was written on Easter 1968, just before Berrigan and his brother Philip, also a Catholic priest, led a raid on the Catonsville, Maryland, draft board on May 9.*

. . . Every book that deals, as this one tries to, with the news about today, finds itself fairly buried before it is born. Last week's omelette. This week is still in the egg shells. I sit here, breaking eggs to make an Easter, to feed the living as I hope, good news for bad. Some ten or twelve of us (the number is still uncertain) will, if all goes well (ill?) take our religious bodies during this week to a draft center in or near Baltimore. There we shall, of purpose and forethought, remove the A-1 files,[1] sprinkle them in the public street with homemade napalm and set them afire. For which act we shall, beyond doubt, be placed behind bars for some portion of our natural lives, in consequence of our inability to live and die content in the plagued city, to say peace peace when there is no peace, to keep the poor poor, the homeless homeless, the thirsty and hungry thirsty and hungry.

Our apologies, good friends, for the fracture of good order, the burning of paper instead of children, the angering of the orderlies in the front parlor of the charnel house. We could not, so help us God, do otherwise. For we are sick at heart, our hearts give us no rest for

---

[1]Young men without either medical or student deferments were assigned "A-1" status by local draft boards, and were subject to being sent to Vietnam.

Daniel Berrigan, *Night Flight to Hanoi: War Diary with 11 Poems* (New York: Harper & Row, 1968), xvi–xix.

thinking of the Land of Burning Children. And for thinking of that other Child, of whom the poet Luke speaks. The infant was taken up in the arms of an old man, whose tongue grew resonant and vatic at the touch of that beauty. And the old man spoke; this child is set for the fall and rise of many in Israel, a sign that is spoken against.

Small consolation; a child born to make trouble, and to die for it, the first Jew (not the last) to be subject of a "definitive solution." He sets up the cross and dies on it; in the Rose Garden of the executive mansion, on the D.C. Mall, in the courtyard of the Pentagon. We see the sign, we read the direction; you must bear with us, for His sake. Or if you will not, the consequences are our own.

For it will be easy, after all, to discredit us. Our record is bad; troublemakers in church and state, a priest married despite his vows, two convicted felons. We have jail records, we have been turbulent, uncharitable, we have failed in love for the brethren, have yielded to fear and despair and pride, often in our lives. Forgive us.

We are no more, when the truth is told, than ignorant beset men, jockeying against all chance, at the hour of death, for a place at the right hand of the dying One.

We act against the law at a time of the Poor Peoples' March, at a time, moreover, when the government is announcing ever more massive paramilitary means to confront disorder in the cities. It is announced that a computerized center is being built in the Pentagon at a cost of some seven million dollars, to offer instant response to outbreaks anywhere in the land; that, moreover, the government takes so serious a view of civil disorder that federal troops with war experience in Vietnam will have first responsibility to quell civil disorder.

The implications of all this must strike horror in the mind of any thinking man. The war in Vietnam is more and more literally being brought home to us. Its inmost meaning strikes the American ghettos: one war, one crime against the poor, waged (largely) by the poor, in servitude to the affluent. We resist and protest this crime.

Finally, we stretch out our hands to our brothers throughout the world. We who are priests, to our fellow priests. All of us who act against the law, turn to the poor of the world, to the Vietnamese, to the victims, to the soldiers who kill and die; for the wrong reasons, for no reason at all, because they were so ordered—by the authorities of that public order which is in effect a massive institutionalized disorder.

We say killing is disorder; life and gentleness and community and unselfishness is the only order we recognize. For the sake of that order, we risk our liberty, our good name. The time is past when good men can remain silent, when obedience can segregate men from public risk, when the poor can die without defense.

We ask our fellow Christians to consider in their hearts a question that has tortured us, night and day, since the war began. How many must die before our voices are heard, how many must be tortured, dislocated, starved, maddened? How long must the world's resources be raped in the service of legalized murder? When, at what point, will you say no to this war?

We have chosen to say, with the gift of our liberty, if necessary of our lives, the violence stops here, the death stops here, the suppression of the truth stops here, the war stops here.

We wish also to place in question by this act all suppositions about normal times, longings for an untroubled life in a somnolent church, that neat timetable of ecclesiastical renewal which, in respect to the needs of men, amounts to another form of time serving.

Redeem the times! The times are inexpressibly evil. Christians pay conscious—indeed religious—tribute to Caesar and Mars; by approval of overkill tactics, by brinkmanship, by nuclear liturgies, by racism, by support of genocide. They embrace their society with all their heart, and abandon the cross. They pay lip service to Christ and military service to the powers of death.

And yet, and yet, the times are inexhaustibly good, solaced by the courage and hope of many. The truth rules, Christ is not forsaken. In a time of death, some men—the resisters, those who work hardily for social change, those who preach and embrace the unpalatable truth— such men overcome death, their lives are bathed in the light of the resurrection, the truth has set them free. In the jaws of death, of contumely, of good and ill report, they proclaim their love of the brethren.

We think of such men, in the world, in our nation, in the churches; and the stone in our breast is dissolved; we take heart once more.

29

NEW YORK RADICAL WOMEN

Principles

1968

New York Radical Women (NYRW) was a key "small group" founded in late 1967 by Shulamith Firestone, who earlier helped found Chicago's Westside group. Lasting through early 1969, NYRW spun off other women's liberation groups, including Redstockings and the Radical Feminists. Many important figures in the women's liberation movement were members of NYRW, including Firestone, author of The Dialectic of Sex; *Kathie Sarachild, consciousness-raising theorist; the prolific writer Ellen Willis; Robin Morgan, editor of* Sisterhood Is Powerful; *and Kate Millett, author of* Sexual Politics, *who made the cover of* Time *magazine in 1970. The rage, sense of sisterhood, and concept of a separate women's history expressed in this selection reflect the new radicalism that these younger women brought to feminism.*

We take the woman's side in everything.

We ask not if something is "reformist," "radical," "revolutionary," or "moral." We ask: is it good for women or bad for women?

We ask not if something is "political." We ask: is it effective? Does it get us closest to what we really want in the fastest way?

We define the best interests of women as the best interests of the poorest, most insulted, most despised, most abused woman on earth. Her lot, her suffering and abuse is the threat that men use against all of us to keep us in line. She is what all women fear being called, fear being treated as and yet what we all really are in the eyes of men. She is Everywoman: ugly, dumb (dumb broad, dumb cunt), bitch, nag, hag, whore, fucking and breeding machine, mother of us all. Until Everywoman is free, no woman will be free. When her beauty and knowledge is revealed and seen, the new day will be at hand.

We are critical of all past ideology, literature and philosophy,

---

Reprinted in Robin Morgan, ed., *Sisterhood Is Powerful: An Anthology of Writings from the Women's Liberation Movement* (New York: Vintage, 1970), 583–84.

products as they are of male supremacist culture. We are re-examining even our words, language itself.

We take as our source the hitherto unrecognized culture of women, a culture which from long experience of oppression developed an intense appreciation for life, a sensitivity to unspoken thoughts and the complexity of simple things, a powerful knowledge of human needs and feelings.

We regard our feelings as our most important source of political understanding.

We see the key to our liberation in our collective wisdom and our collective strength.

30

NEW YORK RADICAL WOMEN

No More Miss America!

August 1968

The demonstration at the 1968 Miss America pageant made the women's liberation movement visible nationally through a flurry of media coverage. NYRW organizers set up a "Freedom Trash Can" outside the hall and threw away objects representing the objectification of women's bodies. Inside, activists disrupted the pageant. It is important, given how this protest led to the myth of feminists as "bra burners," to understand its goals. The women involved had grown up with rigidly enforced gender conformity in which even leftist men dismissed their concerns as "chick lib." Like activists in other movements, they planned a highly visual confrontation with a symbolic representation of their oppression. Experience had taught them that this was the only kind of protest that would attract attention. Though criticized by other feminists for insulting the contestants, they sought to show that pageants of semi-naked young white women were linked to military patriotism and the war, as well as to institutionalized racism. And just like the Black Panthers, their leaflet had "Ten Points."

Reprinted in Robin Morgan, ed., *Sisterhood Is Powerful: An Anthology of Writings from the Women's Liberation Movement* (New York: Vintage, 1970), 584–88.

On September 7th in Atlantic City, the Annual Miss America Pageant will again crown "your ideal." But this year, reality will liberate the contest auction-block in the guise of "genyooine" de-plasticized, breathing women. Women's Liberation Groups, black women, high-school and college women, women's peace groups, women's welfare and social-work groups, women's job-equality groups, pro–birth control and pro-abortion groups—women of every political persuasion—all are invited to join us in a day-long boardwalk-theater event, starting at 1:00 P.M. on the Boardwalk in front of Atlantic City's Convention Hall. We will protest the image of Miss America, an image that oppresses women in every area in which it purports to represent us. There will be: Picket Lines; Guerrilla Theater; Leafleting; Lobbying Visits to the contestants urging our sisters to reject the Pageant Farce and join us; a huge Freedom Trash Can (into which we will throw bras, girdles, curlers, false eyelashes, wigs, and representative issues of *Cosmopolitan, Ladies' Home Journal, Family Circle,* etc.—bring any such woman-garbage you have around the house); we will also announce a Boycott of all those commercial products related to the Pageant, and the day will end with a Women's Liberation rally at midnight when Miss America is crowned on live television. Lots of other surprises are being planned (come and add your own!) but we do not plan heavy disruptive tactics and so do not expect a bad police scene. It should be a groovy day on the Boardwalk in the sun with our sisters. In case of arrests, however, we plan to reject all male authority and demand to be busted by policewomen only. (In Atlantic City, women cops are not permitted to make arrests—dig that!)

Male chauvinist-reactionaries on this issue had best stay away, nor are male liberals welcome in the demonstrations. But sympathetic men can donate money as well as cars and drivers.

Male reporters will be refused interviews. We reject patronizing reportage. *Only newswomen will be recognized.*

The Ten Points

We Protest:

1. *The Degrading Mindless-Boob-Girlie Symbol.* The Pageant contestants epitomize the roles we are all forced to play as women. The parade down the runway blares the metaphor of the 4-H Club county fair, where the nervous animals are judged for teeth, fleece, etc., and where the best "specimen" gets the blue ribbon. So are women in our

society forced daily to compete for male approval, enslaved by ludicrous "beauty" standards we ourselves are conditioned to take seriously.

2. *Racism with Roses.* Since its inception in 1921, the Pageant has not had one Black finalist, and this has not been for a lack of test-case contestants. There has never been a Puerto Rican, Alaskan, Hawaiian, or Mexican-American winner. Nor has there ever been a *true* Miss America—an American Indian.

3. *Miss America as Military Death Mascot.* The highlight of her reign each year is a cheerleader-tour of American troops abroad—last year she went to Vietnam to pep-talk our husbands, fathers, sons and boyfriends into dying and killing with a better spirit. She personifies the "unstained patriotic American womanhood our boys are fighting for." The Living Bra and the Dead Soldier. We refuse to be used as Mascots for Murder.

4. *The Consumer Con-Game.* Miss America is a walking commercial for the Pageant's sponsors. Wind her up and she plugs your product on promotion tours and TV—all in an "honest, objective" endorsement. What a shill.

5. *Competition Rigged and Unrigged.* We deplore the encouragement of an American myth that oppresses men as well as women: the win-or-you're-worthless competitive disease. The "beauty contest" creates only one winner to be "used" and forty-nine losers who are "useless."

6. *The Woman as Pop Culture Obsolescent Theme.* Spindle, mutilate, and then discard tomorrow. What is so ignored as last year's Miss America? This only reflects the gospel of our society, according to Saint Male: women must be young, juicy, malleable—hence age discrimination and the cult of youth. And we women are brainwashed into believing this ourselves!

7. *The Unbeatable Madonna-Whore Combination.* Miss America and Playboy's centerfold are sisters over the skin. To win approval, we must be both sexy and wholesome, delicate but able to cope, demure yet titillatingly bitchy. Deviation of any sort brings, we are told, disaster: "You won't get a man!!"

8. *The Irrelevant Crown on the Throne of Mediocrity.* Miss America represents what women are supposed to be: unoffensive, bland, apolitical. If you are tall, short, over or under what weight The Man prescribes you should be, forget it. Personality, articulateness, intelligence, commitment—unwise. Conformity is the key to the crown—and, by extension, to success in our society.

9. *Miss America as Dream Equivalent To—?* In this reputedly democratic society, where every little boy supposedly can grow up to be President, what can every little girl hope to grow [up] to be? Miss America. That's where it's at. Real power to control our own lives is restricted to men, while women get patronizing pseudopower, an ermine cloak and a bunch of flowers; men are judged by their actions, women by their appearance.

10. *Miss America as Big Sister Watching You.* The Pageant exercises Thought Control, attempts to sear the Image onto our minds, to further make women oppressed and men oppressors; to enslave us all the more in high-heeled, low-status roles; to inculcate false values in young girls; to use women as beasts of buying; to seduce us to prostitute ourselves before our own oppression.

NO MORE MISS AMERICA

31

THIRD WORLD LIBERATION FRONT

The Politics of the Strike

1968

This leaflet was issued by Berkeley's Third World Liberation Front at the height of the strike for student-controlled ethnic studies programs. The strike was led in large part by the Asian American Political Association, which began at San Francisco State University and was the first Asian students group. It became a model for many others around the country. The difference between 1964 and 1968 shows how rapidly student politics had moved to the left. In 1964, Berkeley students had led the nationwide fight for student rights with the Free Speech Movement. Only four years later, newly admitted students of color insisted that their struggle was linked to a worldwide anti-imperialist revolution.

Reprinted in Steve Louie and Glenn Omatsu, eds., *Asian Americans: The Movement and the Moment* (Los Angeles: UCLA Asian American Studies Center Press, 2001), 281.

Self-Determination

The fundamental issue of this strike is the right of Third World people to determine the structure and content of the Third World programs on this campus. Although the Administration has granted some of the demands, it has insisted on maintaining control over Third World programs. Third World people have been allowed to play only an advisory role in the decision-making process. Thus, if the Administration disagrees with the type of program that is proposed (e.g., if it is too radical), it will reject that program. We of the Third World feel that we have the right to be able to decide for ourselves what courses and faculty are relevant to our lives. We don't need to be told what to think or how to do it; we are capable of determining on our own what kind of education we want and need. We must have the right to determine our own destiny!

Time and time again, the administration has proven that its interests are not the same as ours and that it cannot be trusted to implement the kind of programs that is [*sic*] relevant to us. We decided that we had made a mistake in relying on the Administrators to grant us the power of self-determination. We recognize that the racist power structure does not give up power willingly. Rights are not given; they must be won. We of the Third World now stand together in the fight for educational freedom in this racist society.

Racism as exemplified in the policies and structure of the university is not just a product of the consciousness of individual man [*sic*] or groups of individuals. Rather, individual or institutional racism flows from a system, capitalism, which profits and perpetuates it. To expose the racist nature of the university, we must explain and defend the principle which cannot only smash racism, but in the long run through revolutionary struggle the system itself. That principle is our right to self determination in all aspects of our lives, from education to the place of work.

The right of Third World People to self determination is a central part of the world-wide conflict against imperialism. That principle is as important to Berkeley as it is to the revolutionary struggle of the peoples in Africa, Asia, and Latin America. Flowing from that principle, THIRD WORLD PEOPLE HAVE THE RIGHT TO DETERMINE THEIR OWN DEMANDS, THEIR OWN STRATEGIES, AND THEIR OWN TACTICS.

32

MIKE KLONSKY

Toward a Revolutionary Youth Movement

December 23, 1968

Mike Klonsky was national secretary of SDS in 1968. Like many radical students in the antiwar movement, he saw the Vietnam War as the logical result of a fundamentally racist and imperialist United States. Increasingly, SDS's leadership identified with the Black Panthers and the third world, calling themselves "revolutionary communists" and emulating leaders like China's Mao Zedong, Cuba's Fidel Castro, and Vietnam's Ho Chi Minh. Here Klonsky argues that campus-based activism must be rejected and that SDS should link up with working class people to build the revolution. Klonsky and others formed the Revolutionary Youth Movement faction of SDS. Some left to create the underground Weatherman group. Others went into the New Communist Movement, made up of many small organizations, such as the Communist Party (Marxist-Leninist), which Klonsky headed in the 1970s.

"... How should we judge whether a youth is revolutionary? ... If today he integrates himself with the masses ... then today he is a revolutionary. If tomorrow he ceases to do so or turns around to oppress the common people, then he becomes a nonrevolutionary or a counterrevolutionary." — Mao Tse-tung [now spelled Mao Zedong].

At this point in history, SDS is faced with its most crucial ideological decision, that of determining its direction with regards to the working class. At this time there must be a realization on the part of many in our movement that students alone cannot and will not be able to bring about the downfall of capitalism, the system which is at the root of man's oppression. Many of us are going to have to go through important changes, personally. As students, we have been indoctrinated with many racist and anti-working-class notions that in turn have produced racism and class-chauvinism in SDS and [were] responsible largely for

New Left Notes, December 23, 1968.

the student-power focus which our movement has had for many years. Student power at this stage of our movement has to be seen as economism: that is, organizing people around a narrow definition of self-interest as opposed to class-interest. We are moving beyond this now, but that movement must be planned carefully and understood by all.

The fact that we saw ourselves as students as well as radicals and accepted that classification of ourselves and many of the false privileges that went along with it (2-S deferment,[1] promise of the "good life" upon graduation, etc.) was primarily responsible for the reactionary tendencies in SDS.

The main task now is to begin moving beyond the limitations of struggle placed upon a student movement. We must realize our potential to reach out to new constituencies both on and off campus and build SDS into a youth movement that is revolutionary.

The notion that we must remain simply "an anti-imperialist student organization" is no longer viable. The nature of our struggle is such that it necessitates an organization that is made up of youth and not just students, and that these youth become class conscious. This means that our struggles must be integrated into the struggles of working people. . . .

The implementation part of this proposal should not be seen as a national program of action but rather as some suggested actions as well as some necessary actions to be taken if such a youth movement is to be built.

1. Build class consciousness in the student movement in the development towards a revolutionary youth movement.
   a. SDS organizers should direct the focus of their energies to organizing on campuses of working-class colleges, community schools, trade schools and technical schools as well as high schools and junior colleges.
   b. Attacks should also focus on the university as an arm of the corporations that exploit and oppress workers. Corporations that exploit workers should be fought on campus. (Aside from producing napalm, Dow Chemical Co. has plants in 27 countries of the third world and is among the largest international corporations.)
   c. SDS should move towards the building of alliances with

---

[1]A 2-S deferment was an automatic exemption from the draft granted to all full-time male college students.

non-academic employees on the campus based on struggle against the common enemy—the university. SDS should view the university as a corporation that directly oppresses the working class.

d. SDS should move to "destudentize" other students by attacking the false privileges of the university, e.g., the 2-S deferment should be attacked on that basis.

e. Some of us should move into factories and shops as well as into working-class communities, to better understand the material oppression of industrial workers, as well as to eradicate prejudices against workers.

f. We should move into the liberation struggle now being fought inside the armed forces and take an active part. Up until now, we have paid only lip service to that struggle of mostly working-class youth.

g. Youth should be made to see their own struggle and the struggle of the Vietnamese against imperialism as the same struggle. The war *must* continue to be an important focus for SDS organizing.

h. We must join the fight against the class and racist nature of the public school system.

i. Drop-out and forced-out youth both should be encouraged to join our movement. . . .

33

THIRD WORLD WOMEN'S ALLIANCE

Equal to What?

1969

Despite the frequent assertion that women's liberation was a movement of white middle-class women, women of color articulated their own brand of feminism. In 1968, SNCC's Black Women's Liberation Committee was formed. Led by Frances Beal, it broadened its scope and renamed

Reprinted in Rosalyn Baxandall and Linda Gordon, eds., *Dear Sisters: Dispatches from the Women's Liberation Movement* (New York: Basic Books, 2000), 65–66.

itself the Third World Women's Alliance (TWWA) in 1969. The TWWA insisted that for women of color and poor women, there could be no liberation without confronting issues of race and class. It also questioned the feminist orthodoxy that a natural sisterhood united all women, pointing out that some forms of women's liberation would merely give white women the opportunity to participate in racial privilege along with white men. Other important organizations of women of color were founded in the 1970s, including the National Black Feminist Organization and the Combahee River Collective.

The Third World Women's Alliance started about December, 1968. Within SNCC (Student Nonviolent Coordinating Committee) a Black women's liberation committee was established and a number of women who had been meeting over a period of a few months decided that we would be drawing in women from other organizations, and that we would be attracting welfare mothers, community workers, and campus radicals — so we decided to change the name to the Black Women's Alliance. As of now, the organization is independent of SNCC and at the same time SNCC has decided to retain its women's caucus.

We decided to form a Black women's organization for many reasons. One was and still is, the widespread myth and concept in the Black community of the matriarchy. We stated that the concept of the matriarchy was a myth and that it has never existed. Our position would be to expose this myth. There was also the widespread concept that by some miracle the oppression of slavery for the Black woman was not as degrading, not as horrifying, not as barbaric. However, we state that in any society where men are not yet free, women are less free because we are further enslaved by our sex.

Now we noticed another interesting thing. And that is, that with the rise of Black nationalism and the rejection of white middle class norms and values, that this rejection of whiteness — white cultures, white norms and values — took a different turn when it came to the Black woman. That is, Black men defined the role of black women in the movement. They stated that our role was a supportive one; others stated that we must become breeders and provide an army; still others stated that we had kotex power or pussy power.[1] We opposed

---

[1]Several Black Panther leaders were known for using these terms to denigrate the women's movement.

these concepts also stating that a true revolutionary movement enhances the status of women.

Now one of the changes that have taken place in the organization, is that we recognize the need for Third World solidarity. That is, we could not express support for Asia, Africa and Latin America and at the same time, ignore non-Black Third World sisters in this country. We found that we would be much more effective and unified by becoming a Third World Women's organization. So our group is opened to all Third World sisters because our oppression is basically caused by the same factors and our enemy is the same. The name of the organization has been changed to reflect this new awareness and composition of the group—THIRD WORLD WOMEN'S ALLIANCE.

Some women in the movement cannot understand why we exclude whites from our meetings and program. The argument that we are all equally oppressed as women and should unite as one big family to confront the system is as artificial as the argument that Third World women should be fighting on only one front.

And to the white women's liberation groups we say . . . until you can deal with your own racism and until you can deal with your OWN poor white sisters, you will never be a liberation movement and you cannot expect to unite with Third World peoples in a common struggle.

Most white women involved in liberation groups come from a middle-class and student thing. They don't address themselves to the problems of poor and working class women, so there is no way in the world they would be speaking for Third World women. There are serious questions that white women must address themselves to. They call for equality. We answer, equal to what? Equal to white men in their power and ability to oppress Third World people??

It is difficult for Third World women to address themselves to the petty problems of who is going to take out the garbage, when there isn't enough food in the house for anything to be thrown away. Fighting for the day-to-day existence of a family and as humans is the struggle of the Third World woman. We are speaking of oppression, we don't need reforms that will put white women into a position to oppress women of color or OUR MEN in much the same way as white men have been doing for centuries. We need changes in the system and attitudes of people that will guarantee the right to live free from hunger, poverty, and racism. Revolution and not reform is the answer.

34

YOUNG LORDS PARTY

Thirteen Point Program and Platform

1969

Originally the New York branch of a Chicago gang that took up radical politics, the Young Lords Party (YLP) evolved into a Puerto Rican revolutionary nationalist group with branches in New York City; Newark, New Jersey; Philadelphia; and Connecticut. The YLP resembled the Black Panther Party in its community service programs and paramilitary style, and its Thirteen Point Program was clearly modeled on the Panthers' Ten-Point Program. The Young Lords' pride in being Puerto Rican and their willingness to defy the police won them support in el barrio, Puerto Rican urban neighborhoods. Unlike the Black Panthers, however, the Young Lords had a notable commitment to women's liberation. After 1972, the YLP merged into the New Communist Movement, becoming the Puerto Rican Revolutionary Workers Organization, and declined rapidly.

1. *We want self-determination for Puerto Ricans, liberation on the island and inside the United States.*

For 500 years, first spain and then the united states have colonized our country. Billions of dollars in profits leave our country for the united states every year. In every way we are slaves of the gringo. We want liberation and the Power in the hands of the People, not Puerto Rican exploiters. QUE VIVA PUERTO RICO LIBRE! [Long live free Puerto Rico!]

2. *We want self-determination for all Latinos.*

Our Latin Brothers and Sisters, inside and outside the united states, are oppressed by amerikkkan[1] business. The Chicano people built the

---

[1] "Amerikkkan" was a spelling used by some radicals to underline the racist (as in KKK, or Ku Klux Klan) nature of U.S. society. Others spelled America with a *k* (Amerika), the German spelling, to suggest a link between American imperialism and Nazism (see Document 35).

Reprinted in Michael Abramson and the Young Lords Party, *Pa'Lante: The Young Lords Party* (New York: McGraw-Hill, 1971), 150.

Southwest, and we support their right to control their lives and their land. The people of Santo Domingo [Dominican Republic] continue to fight against gringo domination and its puppet generals. The armed liberation struggles in Latin America are part of the war of Latinos against imperialism. QUE VIVA LA RAZA! [Long live the Race!]

3. We want liberation of all Third World People.

Just as Latins first slaved under spain and the yanquis, Black people, Indians, and Asians slaved to build the wealth of this country. For 400 years they have fought for freedom and dignity against racist Babylon. Third World people have led the fight for freedom. All the colored and oppressed peoples of the world are one nation under oppression. NO PUERTO RICAN IS FREE UNTIL ALL PEOPLE ARE FREE!

4. We are Revolutionary Nationalists and oppose racism.

The Latin, Black, Indian and Asian people inside the u.s. are colonies fighting for liberation. We know that washington, wall street, and city hall will try to make our nationalism into racism; but Puerto Ricans are of all colors and we resist racism. Millions of poor white people are rising up to demand freedom and we support them. These are the ones in the u.s. that are stepped on by the rulers and the government. We each organize our people, but our fights are the same against oppression and we will defeat it together. POWER TO ALL OPPRESSED PEOPLE!

5. We want equality for women. Down with machismo and male chauvinism.

Under capitalism, women have been oppressed by both society and our men. The doctrine of machismo has been used by men to take out their frustrations on wives, sisters, mothers, and children. Men must fight along with sisters in the struggle for economic and social equality and must recognize that sisters make up over half of the revolutionary army: sisters and brothers are equals fighting for our people. FORWARD SISTERS IN THE STRUGGLE!

6. We want community control of our institutions and land.

We want control of our communities by our people and programs to guarantee that all institutions serve the needs of our people. People's control of police, health services, churches, schools, housing, transportation and welfare are needed. We want an end to attacks on our land by urban renewal, highway destruction, and university corporations. LAND BELONGS TO ALL THE PEOPLE!

7. *We want a true education of our Afro-Indio culture and Spanish language.*

We must learn our long history of fighting against cultural, as well as economic genocide by the spaniards and now the yanquis. Revolutionary culture, culture of our people, is the only true teaching. JIBARO SI, YANQUI NO!

8. *We oppose capitalists and alliances with traitors.*

Puerto Rican rulers, or puppets of the oppressor, do not help our people. They are paid by the system to lead our people down blind alleys, just like the thousands of poverty pimps who keep our communities peaceful for business, or the street workers who keep gangs divided and blowing each other away. We want a society where the people socialistically control their leader. VENCEREMOS! [We will overcome!]

9. *We oppose the amerikkkan military.*

We demand immediate withdrawal of all u.s. military forces and bases from Puerto Rico, VietNam, and all oppressed communities inside and outside the u.s. No Puerto Rican should serve in the u.s. army against his Brothers and Sisters, for the only true army of oppressed people is the People's Liberation Army to fight all rulers. U.S. OUT OF VIETNAM, FREE PUERTO RICO NOW!

10. *We want freedom for all political prisoners and prisoners of war.*

No Puerto Rican should be in jail or prison, first because we are a nation, and amerikkka has no claims on us; second, because we have not been tried by our own people (peers). We also want all freedom fighters out of jail, since they are prisoners of the war for liberation. FREE ALL POLITICAL PRISONERS AND PRISONERS OF WAR!

11. *We are internationalists.*

Our people are brainwashed by television, radio, newspapers, schools and books to oppose people in other countries fighting for their freedom. No longer will we believe these lies, because we have learned who the real enemy is and who our real friends are. We will defend our sisters and brothers around the world who fight for justice and are against the rulers of this country. QUE VIVA CHE GUEVARA! [Long live Che Guevara!]

12. *We believe armed self-defense and armed struggle are the only means to liberation.*

We are oppose[d] to violence—the violence of hungry children, illiterate adults, diseased old people, and the violence of poverty and profit. We have asked, petitioned, gone to courts, demonstrated peacefully, and voted for politicians full of empty promises. But we still ain't free. The time has come to defend the lives of our people against repression and for revolutionary war against the businessmen, politicians, and police. When a government oppresses the people, we have the right to abolish it and create a new one. ARM OURSELVES TO DEFEND OURSELVES!

13. *We want a socialist society.*
We want liberation, clothing, free food, education, health care, transportation, full employment and peace. We want a society where the needs of the people come first, and where we give solidarity and aid to the people of the world, not oppression and racism. HASTA LA VICTORIA SIEMPRE! [Always onward to victory!]

35

MARTHA SHELLEY

Gay Is Good
1969

Martha Shelley was a founder of New York's Gay Liberation Front. She had been active in the Daughters of Bilitis, a lesbian homophile group organized in the 1950s, but was frustrated by its caution. Her satirical, defiant style was typical of the gay liberation movement. At the August 26, 1970, Women's Strike for Equality rally in New York City, Shelley protested the fact that no lesbian had been invited to speak by forcing her way onto the stage to address the crowd. The essay reprinted here, written in 1969, describes the desire to "come out"—to celebrate gayness without worrying about whether it made heterosexuals uneasy. It inspired thousands of gays around the country.

Reprinted in Karla Jay and Allen Young, eds., *Out of the Closets: Voices of Gay Liberation,* 20th anniv. ed. (New York: New York University Press, 1992), 31–34.

Look out, straights. Here comes the Gay Liberation Front, springing up like warts all over the bland face of Amerika, causing shudders of indigestion in the delicately balanced bowels of the movement. Here come the gays, marching with six-foot banners to Washington and embarrassing the liberals, taking over Mayor Alioto's office, staining the good names of War Resisters' League and Women's Liberation by refusing to pass for straight anymore.[1]

We've got chapters in New York, San Francisco, San Jose, Los Angeles, Minneapolis, Philadelphia, Wisconsin, Detroit and I hear maybe even in Dallas. We're gonna make our own revolution because we're sick of revolutionary posters which depict straight he-man types and earth mothers, with guns and babies. We're sick of the Panthers lumping us together with the capitalists in their term of universal contempt—"faggot."

And I am personally sick of liberals who say they don't care who sleeps with whom, it's what you do outside of bed that counts. This is what homosexuals have been trying to get straights to understand for years. Well, it's too late for liberalism. Because what I do outside of bed may have nothing to do with what I do inside—but my consciousness is branded, is permeated with homosexuality. For years I have been branded with *your* label for me. The result is that when I am among gays or in bed with another woman, I am a person, not a lesbian. When I am observable to the straight world, I become gay. You are my litmus paper.

We want something more now, something more than the tolerance you never gave us. But to understand that, you must understand who we are.

We are the extrusions of your unconscious mind—your worst fears made flesh. From the beautiful boys at Cherry Grove[2] to the aging queens in the uptown bars, the taxi-driving dykes to the lesbian fashion models, the hookers (male and female) on 42nd Street, the leather lovers . . . and the very ordinary very un-lurid gays . . . we are the sort of people everyone was taught to despise—and now we are shaking off the chains of self-hatred and marching on your citadels of repression.

---

[1]Joseph Alioto was the Democratic mayor of San Francisco. The War Resisters' League was a long-established pacifist organization that had many covert gay members.

[2]Cherry Grove is a section of Fire Island, a beach resort on New York's Long Island long known as a haven for gays and lesbians.

Liberalism isn't good enough for us. And we are just beginning to discover it. Your friendly smile of acceptance—from the safe position of heterosexuality—isn't enough. As long as you cherish that secret belief that you are a little bit better because you sleep with the opposite sex, you are still asleep in your cradle and we will be the nightmare that awakens you.

We are women and men who, from the time of our earliest memories, have been in revolt against the sex-role structure and nuclear family structure. The roles we have played amongst ourselves, the self-deceit, the compromises and the subterfuges—these have never totally obscured the fact that we exist outside the traditional structure—and our existence threatens it.

Understand this—that the worst part of being a homosexual is having to keep it *secret.* Not the occasional murders by police or teenage queer-beaters, not the loss of jobs or expulsion from schools or dishonorable discharges—but the daily knowledge that what you are is so awful that it cannot be revealed. The violence against us is sporadic. Most of us are not affected. But the internal violence of being made to carry—or choosing to carry—the load of your straight society's unconscious guilt—this is what tears us apart, what makes us want to stand up in the offices, in the factories and schools and shout out our true identities.

We were rebels from our earliest days—somewhere, maybe just about the time we started to go to school, we rejected straight society—unconsciously. Then, later, society rejected us, as we came into full bloom. The homosexuals who hide, who play it straight or pretend that the issue of homosexuality is unimportant, are only hiding the truth from themselves. They are trying to become part of a society that they rejected instinctively when they were five years old, to pretend that it is the result of heredity, or a bad mother, or anything but a gut reaction of nausea against the roles forced on us.

If you are homosexual, and you get tired of waiting around for the liberals to repeal the sodomy laws, and begin to dig yourself—and get angry—you are on your way to being a radical. Get in touch with the reasons that made you reject straight society as a kid (remembering my own revulsion against the vacant women drifting in and out of supermarkets, vowing never to live like them) and realize that you were *right.* Straight roles stink.

And you straights—look down the street, at the person whose sex is not readily apparent. Are you uneasy? Or are you made more uneasy by the stereotype gay, the flaming faggot or diesel dyke? Or most uneasy by the friend you thought was straight—and isn't? We want you to be uneasy, be a little less comfortable in your straight roles. And to make you uneasy, we behave outrageously—even though we pay a heavy price for it—and our outrageous behavior comes out of our rage.

But what is strange to you is natural to us. Let me illustrate. The Gay Liberation Front (GLF) "liberates" a gay bar for the evening. We come in. The people already there are seated quietly at the bar. Two or three couples are dancing. It's a down place. And the GLF takes over. Men dance with men, women with women, men with women, everyone in circles. No roles. You ever see that at a straight party? Not men with men—this is particularly verboten. No, and you're not likely to, while the gays in the movement are still passing for straight in order to keep up the good names of their organizations or to keep up the pretense that they are acceptable—and to have to get out of the organization they worked so hard for.

True, some gays play the same role-games among themselves that straights do. Isn't every minority group fucked over by the values of the majority culture? But the really important thing about being gay is that you are forced to notice how much sex-role differentiation is pure artifice, is nothing but a game.

Once I dressed up for an American Civil Liberties Union benefit. I wore a black lace dress, heels, elaborate hairdo and makeup. And felt like—a drag queen. Not like a woman—I am a woman every day of my life—but like the ultimate in artifice, a woman posing as a drag queen.

The roles are beginning to wear thin. The makeup is cracking. The roles—breadwinner, little wife, screaming fag, bulldyke, James Bond—are the cardboard characters we are always trying to fit into, as if being human and spontaneous were so horrible that we each have to pick on a character out of a third-rate novel and try to cut ourselves down to its size. And you cut off your homosexuality—and we cut off our heterosexuality.

Back to the main difference between us. We gays are separate from you—we are alien. You have managed to drive your own homosexuality down under the skin of your mind—and to drive us down and out into the gutter of self-contempt. We, ever since we became aware of being gay, have each day been forced to internalize the labels: "I am a pervert, a dyke, a fag, etc." And the days pass, until we look at you out of our homosexual bodies, bodies that have become synonymous and consubstantial with homosexuality, bodies that are no longer bodies but labels; and sometimes we wish we were like you, sometimes we wonder how you can stand yourselves.

It's difficult for me to understand how you can dig each other as human beings—in a man-woman relationship—how you can relate to each other in spite of your sex roles. It must be awfully difficult to talk to each other, when the woman is trained to repress what the man is trained to express, and vice-versa. Do straight men and women talk to each other? Or does the man talk and the woman nod approvingly? Is love possible between heterosexuals; or is it all a case of women posing as nymphs, earth-mothers, sex-objects, what-have-you; and men writing the poetry of romantic illusions to these walking stereo-types?

I tell you, the function of a homosexual is to make you uneasy.

And now I will tell you what we want, we radical homosexuals: not for you to tolerate us, or to accept us, but to understand us. And this you can do only by becoming one of us. We want to reach the homo-sexuals entombed in you, to liberate our brothers and sisters, locked in the prisons of your skulls.

We want you to understand what it is to be our kind of outcast— but also to understand our kind of love, to hunger for your own sex. Because unless you understand this, you will continue to look at us with uncomprehending eyes, fake liberal smiles; you will be incapable of loving us.

We will never go straight until you go gay. As long as you divide yourselves, we will be divided from you—separated by a mirror trick of your mind. We will no longer allow you to drop us—or the homo-sexuals in yourselves—into the reject bin; labelled sick, childish or perverted. And because we will not wait, your awakening may be a rude and bloody one. It's your choice. You will never be rid of us, because we reproduce ourselves out of your bodies—and out of your minds. We are one with you.

36

MOVIMIENTO ESTUDIANTIL CHICANO DE AZTLÁN

El Plan de Santa Barbara

April 1969

In April 1969, student leaders from around California formed MEChA, *the* Movimiento Estudiantil Chicano de Aztlán *(Chicano Student Movement of Aztlán—an Indian name for the Southwest). They adopted El Plan de Santa Barbara, embracing "cultural nationalism [as] a means of Chicano liberation." Its ideology of* Chicanismo *insisted on an "ancestral communalism" that predated the European conquest of the New World. The plan's emphasis on using college programs as a tool for community empowerment was common to the new movements among people of color.* MEChA, *like many student organizations, flourished for only a few years in the early 1970s, although it has reappeared periodically and remained a point of reference for Chicano militancy since then.*

Manifesto

For all peoples, as with individuals, the time comes when they must reckon with their history. For the Chicano the present is a time of renaissance, of *renacimiento.* Our people and our community, *el barrio* and *la colonia,*[1] are expressing a new consciousness and a new resolve. Recognizing the historical tasks confronting our people and fully aware of the cost of human progress, we pledge our will to move. We will move forward toward our destiny as a people. We will move against those forces which have denied us freedom of expression and human dignity. Throughout history the quest for cultural expression and freedom has taken the form of a struggle. Our struggle, tempered by the lessons of the American past, is an historical reality.

---

[1]*El barrio* refers to one's immediate neighborhood and *la colonia* means the larger community.

Reprinted in Carlos Muñoz Jr., *Youth, Identity, Power: The Chicano Movement* (London: Verso, 1989), 191–96.

For decades Mexican people in the United States struggled to realize the "American Dream." And some—a few—have. But the cost, the ultimate cost of assimilation, required turning away from *el barrio* and *la colonia*. In the meantime, due to the racist structure of this society, to our essentially different life style, and to the socioeconomic functions assigned to our community by Anglo-American society—as suppliers of cheap labor and a dumping ground for the small-time capitalist entrepreneur—the *barrio* and *colonia* remained exploited, impoverished, and marginal.

As a result, the self-determination of our community is now the only acceptable mandate for social and political action; it is the essence of Chicano commitment. Culturally, the word *Chicano,* in the past a pejorative and class-bound adjective, has now become the root idea of a new cultural identity for our people. It also reveals a growing solidarity and the development of a common social praxis. The widespread use of the term *Chicano* today signals a rebirth of pride and confidence. *Chicanismo* simply embodies an ancient truth: that man is never closer to his true self as when he is close to his community.

Chicanismo draws its faith and strength from two main sources: from the just struggle of our people and from an objective analysis of our community's strategic needs. We recognize that without a strategic use of education, an education that places value on what we value, we will not realize our destiny. Chicanos recognize the central importance of institutions of higher learning to modern progress, in this case, to the development of our community. But we go further: we believe that higher education must contribute to the information of a complete man who truly values life and freedom.

The destiny of our people will be fulfilled. To that end, we pledge our efforts and take as our credo what José Vasconcelos[2] once said at a time of crisis and hope: "At this moment we do not come to work for the university, but to demand that the university work for our people."

Political Action

. . . Commitment to the struggle for Chicano liberation is the operative definition of the ideology used here. *Chicanismo* involves a crucial distinction in political consciousness between a Mexican American and a Chicano mentality. The Mexican American is a person who lacks

---

[2]José Vasconcelos (1882–1959) was a Mexican educator and writer much admired by cultural nationalists, and author of *La Raza Cósmica* (1925).

respect for his cultural and ethnic heritage. Unsure of himself, he seeks assimilation as a way out of his "degraded" social status. Consequently, he remains politically ineffective. In contrast, *Chicanismo* reflects self-respect and pride in one's ethnic and cultural background. Thus, the Chicano acts with confidence and with a range of alternatives in the political world. He is capable of developing an effective ideology through action.

Mexican Americans must be viewed as potential Chicanos. *Chicanismo* is flexible enough to relate to the varying levels of consciousness within *La Raza*.[3] Regional variations must always be kept in mind as well as the different levels of development, composition, maturity, achievement, and experience in political action. Cultural nationalism is a means of total Chicano liberation.

There are definite advantages to cultural nationalism, but no inherent limitations. A Chicano ideology, especially as it involves cultural nationalism, should be positively phrased in the form of propositions to the Movement. *Chicanismo* is a concept that integrates self-awareness with cultural identity, a necessary step in developing political consciousness. As such, it serves as a basis for political action, flexible enough to include the possibility of coalitions. The related concept of *La Raza* provides an internationalist scope of *Chicanismo,* and *La Raza Cósmica*[4] furnishes a philosophical precedent. Within this framework, the Third World Concept merits consideration. . . .

Campus Organizing: Notes on MEChA

. . . MEChA is a first step to tying the student groups throughout the Southwest into a vibrant and responsive network of activists who will respond as a unit to oppression and racism and will work in harmony when initiating and carrying out campaigns of liberation for our people.

As of present, wherever one travels throughout the Southwest, one finds that there are different levels of awareness on different campuses. The student movement is to a large degree a political movement and as such must not elicit from our people the negative

---

[3]*La Raza,* literally "the Race," was a term used by Chicano activists to mean all Mexican people on both sides of the border.

[4]*La Raza Cósmica,* "the Cosmic Race," referred to a belief that the special history of Mexicans, with roots in the New and Old Worlds, gave them a unique destiny.

responses that we have experienced so often in the past in relation to politics, and often with good reason. To this end, then, we must redefine politics for our people to be a means of liberation. The political sophistication of our Raza must be raised so that they do not fall prey to apologists and *vendidos* [sellouts] whose whole interest is their personal career or fortune. In addition, the student movement is more than a political movement, it is cultural and social as well. The spirit of MEChA must be one of "hermandad" [brotherhood] and cultural awareness. The ethic of profit and competition, of greed and intolerance, which the Anglo society offers must be replaced by our ancestral communalism and love for beauty and justice. MEChA must bring to the mind of every young Chicano that the liberation of his people from prejudice and oppression is in his hands and this responsibility is greater than personal achievement and more meaningful than degrees, especially if they are earned at the expense of his identity and cultural integrity.

MEChA, then, is more than a name; it is a spirit of unity, of brotherhood, and a resolve to undertake a struggle for liberation in a society where justice is but a word. MEChA is a means to an end....

37

INDIANS OF ALL TRIBES

Proclamation

November 1969

In November 1969, a coalition of veteran activists and students attending the new Native American studies programs at San Francisco State University and Berkeley took over the unused federal prison on Alcatraz Island in San Francisco Bay. Like other spectacular protests, the occupation of Alcatraz derived energy from considerable media attention, which stimulated support from whites. For instance, the rock band Creedence

Reprinted in Alvin M. Josephy Jr., Joane Nagel, and Troy Johnson, eds., *Red Power: The American Indians' Fight for Freedom,* 2nd ed. (Lincoln: University of Nebraska Press, 1999), 40–43.

*Clearwater Revival donated a boat to bring supplies to the island. The
following proclamation of the island's seizure mocked the status of Native
American reservations under the Bureau of Indian Affairs and asserted
a utopian vision of cultural rebirth. The occupation itself became chaotic
and finally collapsed in June 1971. The vision survived, however, and
inspired an ongoing renaissance of American Indian culture.*

To the Great White Father and All His People:

We, the native Americans, re-claim the land known as Alcatraz
Island in the name of all American Indians by right of discovery.

We wish to be fair and honorable in our dealings with the Caucasian inhabitants of this land, and hereby offer the following treaty:

We will purchase said Alcatraz Island for twenty-four dollars ($24)
in glass beads and red cloth, a precedent set by the white man's purchase of a similar island about 300 years ago. We know that $24 in
trade goods for these 16 acres is more than was paid when Manhattan
Island was sold, but we know that land values have risen over the
years. Our offer of $1.24 per acre is greater than the 47 cents per acre
the white men are now paying the California Indians for their land.

We will give to the inhabitants of this island a portion of that land for
their own, to be held in trust by the American Indian Government—
for as long as the sun shall rise and the rivers go down to the sea—to
be administered by the Bureau of Caucasian Affairs (BCA). We will further guide the inhabitants in the proper way of living. We will offer
them our religion, our education, our life-ways, in order to help them
achieve our level of civilization and thus raise them and all their white
brothers up from their savage and unhappy state. We offer this treaty
in good faith and wish to be fair and honorable in our dealings with all
white men.

We feel that this so-called Alcatraz Island is more than suitable for
an Indian Reservation, as determined by the white man's own standards. By this we mean that this place resembles most Indian reservations, in that:

1. It is isolated from modern facilities, and without adequate
   means of transportation.
2. It has no fresh running water.
3. It has inadequate sanitation facilities.
4. There are no oil or mineral rights.

5. There is no industry so unemployment is great.
6. There are no health care facilities.
7. The soil is rocky and non-productive; and the land does not support game.
8. There are no educational facilities.
9. The population has always exceeded the land base.
10. The population has always been held as prisoners and kept dependent upon others.

Further, it would be fitting and symbolic that ships from all over the world, entering the Golden Gate, would first see Indian land, and thus be reminded of the true history of this nation. This tiny island would be a symbol of the great lands once ruled by free and noble Indians.

Use to Be Made of Alcatraz Island

What use will be made of this land?

Since the San Francisco Indian Center burned down, there is no place for Indians to assemble and carry on our tribal life here in the white man's city. Therefore, we plan to develop on this island several Indian institutes:

1. A Center for Native American Studies will be developed which will train our young people in the best of our native cultural arts and sciences, as well as educate them to the skills and knowledge relevant to improve the lives and spirits of all Indian peoples. Attached to this center will be traveling universities, managed by Indians, which will go to the Indian Reservations in order to learn the traditional values from the people, which are now absent in the Caucasian higher educational system.

2. An American Indian Spiritual center will be developed which will practice our ancient tribal religious ceremonies and medicine. Our cultural arts will be featured and our young people trained in music, dance, and medicine.

3. An Indian center of Ecology will be built which will train and support our young people in scientific research and practice in order to restore our lands and waters to their pure and natural state. We will seek to de-pollute the air and the water of the Bay Area. We will seek to restore fish and animal life, and to revitalize sea life which has been threatened by the white man's way. Facilities will be developed to desalt sea water for human use.

4. A Great Indian Training School will be developed to teach our peoples how to make a living in the world, improve our standards of living, and end hunger and unemployment among all our peoples. This training school will include a center for Indian arts and crafts, and an Indian Restaurant serving native foods and training Indians in culinary arts. This center will display Indian arts and offer the Indian foods of all tribes to the public, so they all may know of the beauty and spirit of the traditional Indian ways.

5. Some of the present buildings will be taken over to develop an American Indian Museum, which will depict our native foods and other cultural contributions we have given to all the world. Another part of the Museum will present some of the things the white man has given to the Indians, in return for the land and the life he took: disease, alcohol, poverty, and cultural decimation (as symbolized by old tin cans, barbed wire, rubber tires, plastic containers, etc.). Part of the museum will remain a dungeon, to symbolize both Indian captives who were incarcerated for challenging white authority, and those who were imprisoned on reservations. The Museum will show the noble and the tragic events of Indian history, including the broken treaties, the documentary of the Trail of Tears, the Massacre of Wounded Knee, as well as the victory over Yellow-Hair Custer and his army.

In the name of all Indians, therefore, we re-claim this island for Indian nations, for all these reasons. We feel this claim is just and proper, and that this land should rightfully be granted to us for as long as the rivers shall run and the sun shall shine.

38

GAY ACTIVISTS ALLIANCE

Preamble to Constitution

December 1969

New York's Gay Activists Alliance (GAA) single-handedly made gay people a force in liberal politics in New York City and then nationwide. It developed strategies that were widely emulated, combining militant actions with a pragmatic agenda of getting antidiscrimination provisions protecting gays into the city's municipal code. The GAA constitution emphasizes its single-issue stance: to unite all homosexuals around a civil rights campaign without requiring or even permitting any other political positions to be discussed. Earlier homophile groups, such as the Mattachine Society, had emphasized respectability and disdained those parts of the gay community (such as drag queens) that heterosexuals most disliked. By contrast, the GAA emphatically welcomed all, regardless of their appearance or sexual preference.

The Gay Activists Alliance is a militant (though nonviolent) homosexual civil rights organization. Membership is open to all persons—male or female, young or old, homosexual and heterosexual—who agree with the purposes of the organization and who are prepared to devote time to their implementation.

GAA is exclusively devoted to the liberation of homosexuals and avoids involvement in any program of action not obviously relevant to homosexuals. Although individual members of GAA are involved in many different social causes, the organization as such is a one-issue organization. GAA adopted this policy in order to win the support of large numbers of homosexuals—regardless of differences in social perspective—and to avoid internal political dispute. This policy is written into the GAA constitution.

GAA is a structured organization. It has officers and committees,

---

Reprinted in Donn Teal, *The Gay Militants: How Gay Liberation Began in America, 1969–1971* (New York: Stein and Day, 1971; repr., New York: St. Martin's Press, 1995), 110–11.

but only the membership can decide upon policy. This is done at our weekly general membership meetings. Meetings are conducted in accordance with parliamentary law. GAA adopted this policy to insure that policy decisions are mutually consistent, arrived at democratically, and carried out efficiently. This policy is also written into the GAA constitution.

GAA is a political organization. Everything is done with an eye toward political effect. Although dances and other social events are sometimes held, their purpose is to raise the political consciousness of the gay community and to contribute to its sense of social solidarity. GAA adopted this policy because all oppression of homosexuals is based on political oppression and because the liberation of homosexuals can only be effected by means of a powerful political bloc.

GAA uses the tactics of confrontation politics. Politicians and persons of authority in society who contribute to the oppression of homosexuals are publicly exposed through mass demonstrations, disruption of meetings, and sit-ins. GAA adopted this policy because the first necessary stage in homosexual liberation is the development of an open sense of public identity in the gay community and a corresponding sense of fear and embarrassment in the government.

GAA does not endorse any candidate for public office or any political party. The response of politicians to GAA confrontations—whether a favorable or an unfavorable response—is given the widest possible circulation in the straight and gay press, but the organization as such does not commit itself to anyone's political career. GAA adopted this policy to avoid compromising entanglements within the political system. This policy is written into the GAA constitution.

GAA is open to all varieties of homosexual culture. No member may be discriminated against because of personal appearance, style of behavior, or sexual taste. GAA adopted this policy because prejudice against sub-minorities within the gay community is inconsistent with the struggle for fundamental human rights. . . .

39

AMERICAN CIVIL LIBERTIES UNION

On the Record of Police Actions against the Black Panther Party: Press Release

December 29, 1969

From 1968 on, as police harassment and killing of Black Panthers and other radicals increased, journalists and civil liberties groups investigated what looked like persecution. These exposés reflected a fear that police forces and the Nixon administration were becoming uncontrollable. This press release from the American Civil Liberties Union (ACLU), the major national organization defending constitutional freedoms, reported that there was a clear pattern of harassment, infiltration, and entrapment regarding the Black Panther Party. It included statements by top administration officials that clearly condoned violent repression of the party. Liberal concern kept some activists out of jail or alive but was otherwise ineffective in preventing government agencies from repressing and breaking up radical groups.

"The record of police actions across the country against the Black Panther Party forms a prima facie case for the conclusion that law enforcement officials are waging a drive against the black militant organization resulting in serious civil liberties violations," the American Civil Liberties Union said today.

"First Amendment and due process guarantees have been breached in numerous instances," the ACLU reported in disclosing a spot check survey of ACLU affiliate offices in 9 major metropolitan centers.

The national survey, prompted by the recent Chicago and Los Angeles police raids on Black Panther officials, suggests that a pattern of harassment exists and describes the nature of the civil liberties violations involved. ACLU affiliates, in individual cases, have defended

Reprinted in Philip S. Foner, ed., *The Black Panthers Speak: The Manifesto of the Party: The First Complete Documentary Record of the Panthers' Program* (Philadelphia: J. B. Lippincott, 1970), 263–65.

the rights of Black Panther groups when civil liberties issues have arisen.

"Quite aside from the killing of Panthers and police which we abhor, ACLU affiliates have reported that the style of law enforcement applied to Black Panthers has amounted to provocative and even punitive harassment, defying the constitutional rights of Panthers to make political speeches or distribute political literature.

"In San Francisco, Los Angeles, Chicago, Philadelphia and New York, police have made repeated arrests of Panthers for distributing papers without a permit, harassment, interfering with an officer, loitering and disorderly conduct—stemming from incidents where police have challenged Panthers as they attempted to distribute their newspaper or other political materials. Seldom have these charges held up in court, often they have been dropped by the prosecutor prior to trial, and in one New York case the arresting officer acknowledged that he had no evidence but had been instructed to 'get on the books' the arrest of a particular Panther who was already on the books of an adjoining county. We view this style of law enforcement as applied with prejudice to the Panthers, as inflammatory, and very susceptible to escalation into violent confrontations.

"ACLU affiliates in New York and Indiana report infiltration by government informants into black groups thought to be Panthers for the purpose of entrapment. The evidence indicates that government agents have attempted to induce black militants to burglarize, in one case offering automatic weapons, in another providing a map of the likely target, a getaway car and the offer of weapons. This is an abominable tactic for officers of the law to undertake. Police are supposed to prevent crimes, not encourage them.

"A common police procedure reported to us by ACLU affiliates in New York, Pennsylvania, Connecticut, Illinois, Indiana, California and Wisconsin is that of excessive traffic stops by police of Black Panther Party members. These challenges by police are so frequent in number and so forceful in manner as to be unconstitutional. They have rarely resulted in traffic violations, arrest of a known fugitive or charges of illegal possession of weapons. They more often produce the traditional catch-all charges of the police roust—disorderly conduct, interference with an officer, resisting arrest.

"Other police actions which bear out charges of harassment are reported from Chicago where police and FBI agents undertook a June 4th dawn raid on Panther headquarters with an arrest warrant for

George Sams, but no search warrant. Upon smashing down the door of the office and failing to find George Sams, enforcement officials broke up furniture, confiscated literature, lists of donors and petitions and arrested eight Panthers on charges so flimsy they were later dismissed. The following day a similar raid was made in Detroit, the door broken down, documents photographed, three Panthers arrested on specious charges and later released.

"Our reports do not prove a directed national campaign to get the Panthers. However, even if not a concerted program of harassment, high national officials, by their statements and actions, have helped to create the climate of oppression and have encouraged local police to initiate the crackdowns. For example, the Vice President has called the Panthers a 'completely irresponsible, anarchistic group of criminals'; the Assistant Attorney General, Jerris Leonard, has said, 'The Black Panthers are nothing but hoodlums and we've got to get them'; FBI Director J. Edgar Hoover has called the Panthers 'the greatest threat to the internal security of the country [among] violence-prone black-extremist groups'; and Attorney General John N. Mitchell has ruled that the Panthers are a threat to national security, thus subject to FBI surveillance by wiretapping.

"This official federal posture makes it easy for the president of the Cleveland Fraternal Order of Police to suggest, 'the country doesn't need the Black Panther Party, to my way of thinking, they need to be wiped out.'

"We believe the climate of anger and the specific cases of police harassment against the Black Panther Party warrant intensive investigation. We are therefore consolidating the case materials, letters and notes from ACLU affiliates for submission to the Commission of Inquiry into the Black Panthers and Law Enforcement Officials convened by 28 eminent Americans and national organizations and headed by former U.S. Supreme Court Justice Arthur Goldberg. The ACLU is a participating organization in the Inquiry." . . .

40

KATHIE SARACHILD

Outline for Consciousness-Raising

1970

A founding member of New York Radical Women, Kathie Sarachild (born Amatniek, she changed her name to honor her mother) later formed another important "small group," the Radical Feminists. She was the principal exponent of consciousness-raising as an organizing technique. This guide to organizing a local group was widely circulated in 1968–69 and appeared in the extremely influential anthology Sisterhood Is Powerful *in 1970. It outlines the stages a group of women might go through over several months, from individual self-exploration to shared conclusions leading to a theoretical analysis of women's oppression. Although many women simply started groups after hearing about them or reading this outline, each consciousness-raising group was encouraged to spawn others.*

I. The "bitch session" cell group
   A. Ongoing consciousness expansion
      1. Personal recognition and testimony
      2. Personal testimony—methods of group practice
         a. Going around the room with key questions on key topics
         b. Speaking out experience at random
         c. Cross-examination
      3. Relating and generalizing individual testimony
   B. Classic forms of resisting consciousness, *or* How to avoid facing the awful truth:
   Including
         Anti-womanism
         Glorification of the Oppressor
         Excusing or Feeling Sorry for the Oppressor

Reprinted in Robin Morgan, ed., *Sisterhood Is Powerful: An Anthology of Writings from the Women's Liberation Movement* (New York: Vintage, 1970), xxvi–xxvii.

Romantic Fantasies
"An Adequate Personal Solution"
Self-cultivation, Rugged Individualism
Self-blame
Ultra-militancy, etc.
C. "Starting to stop"—overcoming repressions and delusions
  a. Reasons for repressing one's own consciousness
    1. Fear of feeling one's past wasted and meaningless
    2. Fear of despair for the future, etc.
  b. Analyzing which fears are valid and which invalid
  c. Discussing possible methods of struggle in a historical context, an individual context, and a group context. Daring to share one's experiences with the group
D. Understanding and developing radical feminist theory
  Using the above techniques to begin to understand our oppression
  Analyzing whatever privileges we have; white skin, education, class, etc. and see how these help perpetuate our oppression and that of others
E. Consciousness-raiser (organizer) training—so that every woman in a given "bitch session" cell group herself becomes an "organizer" in turn, of other groups
II. Consciousness-raising actions
III. Organizing
  Helping new people start groups
  Intra-group communication and actions
  Monthly meetings
  Conferences

41

TOM GRACE

Remembering the Killings at Kent State
1987

The May 1970 shootings at Kent State University in Ohio exemplify the polarization of U.S. society wrought by the Vietnam War. After President Nixon's invasion of Cambodia on April 30, many college campuses were in a virtual state of war. At Kent, protesters firebombed the ROTC building and threatened more disruption. Governor James Rhodes sent in the poorly trained National Guard. On the afternoon of May 4, they fired their automatic rifles into a crowd without warning, killing four and wounding nine; several of those who were shot were just walking to class. Although the killings gave a sense of desperate urgency to the antiwar movement, a majority of Americans told pollsters that they supported the Guardsmen's actions. Lost was how the students themselves—the protesters, spectators, and friends of the wounded and killed—felt. Tom Grace was a student who joined the protest and got shot in the foot.

My first class of the day was at nine-fifty-five and my girlfriend was in the same class. Because of all the tumultuous disorder that had gone on for the preceding days, the professor, being an understanding man, gave people the option of leaving and taking the exam at another time if the events had interfered with their studying, or going ahead and taking the test. . . .

Toward the end of the class, I recall a student standing and saying that there was going to be a rally on the commons as soon as the class was over. I sat there for a few minutes deliberating as to whether I should go or not. . . . Then I thought to myself, This is too momentous; it's too important for me to stay away. Certainly I couldn't see any harm in my going over just to watch. So I went over there really with the intention of more or less surveying the scene, not knowing what I was going to find.

Reprinted in Joan Morrison and Robert K. Morrison, eds., *From Camelot to Kent State* (New York: Times Books, 1987), 329–34.

It was only a short five-minute walk to the commons. I found several hundred students, and some of my roommates, Alan Canfora and Jim Riggs, had flags, black flags, I believe. Alan had spray-painted "KENT" on it, and the other one was just a black flag, and they were waving these things about. So I was drawn to them right away. There was some chanting going on: "One, two, three, four, we don't want your fucking war" and "Pigs off campus."

The crowd had grouped around the victory bell, which had been historically used to signal victories in Kent State football games, and the bell was being sounded to signal students to congregate. There were at the very least another thousand or so observers and onlookers ringing the hills that surround this part of the commons.

At that point, a campus policeman in a National Guard jeep ordered the crowd, through the use of a bullhorn, to disperse and go to their homes. The policeman was riding shotgun, and I believe a National Guardsman was driving the jeep. "All you bystanders and innocent people go to your homes for your own safety," is what we heard. I think he had the best of intentions in terms of asking the crowd to disperse, but it did nothing but whip the crowd into a further frenzy.

We have to remember here the mind-set of people and everything that had gone on. A very adversarial atmosphere existed, and we felt that this was our campus, that we were doing nothing wrong, and that they had no right to order us to disperse. If anyone ought to leave, it's them, not us. That's how I felt.

I was standing there yelling and screaming along with everyone else, and then someone flung either a rock or a bottle at the jeep, which bounced harmlessly off the tire. I don't think it was necessarily meant to bounce off the tire; fortunately the person was not a very good shot. That, of course, alarmed the occupants of the jeep. I think they realized at that point—because of the crescendo the chants had reached, and also the fact that people were pitching objects in their direction—that we weren't going to leave.

So the jeep drove back to the National Guard lines which had formed on the other side of the commons in front of the remains of the burned ROTC building. Then the National Guardsmen leveled their bayonets at us and started to march across the commons in our direction, shooting tear gas as they came.

I was teargassed along with perhaps a thousand other people. Unlike some of the students, who delayed to throw rocks or tear-gas cannisters back in the direction of the National Guard, I chose to leave the area as fast as I could. I retreated to a girls' dormitory where there were some first-floor restrooms. The female students had opened up the windows and were passing out moistened paper towels so people could relieve the effects of the tear gas. So I went and I cleansed my eyes to the best of my ability, and that seemed to take care of me at the moment.

In the meantime, one group of National Guardsmen had advanced the same way that I had retreated, but they did not chase the students further. But another troop of the National Guard had gone right past and proceeded downhill onto the practice football field. There was a rather abrupt drop-off and a chain-link fence where some construction had been going on, and on the other three sides the National Guardsmen were ringed by students.

I cautiously moved a little closer and watched. Some students were throwing rocks at the National Guard, and some of the National Guard were picking up the rocks and throwing them back at the students. I didn't see any National Guardsmen hit by rocks. They seemed to be bouncing at their feet.

Then I remember that the National Guard troop seemed to get into a little huddle before leaving the practice football field. They reformed their lines and proceeded back up the hill. It was almost like the parting of the Red Sea. The students just moved to one side or the other to let the National Guardsmen pass, because no one in their right mind would have stood there as bayonets were coming.

A lot of people were screaming, "Get out of here, get off our campus," and in the midst of all this were some students, oddly enough, who were still wandering through the area with their textbooks, as if they were completely unaware of all that was taking place. I felt that I was still keeping a safe distance. I was 150, 165 feet away. I know that because it's since been paced off.

When the National Guardsmen got to the top of the hill, all of a sudden there was just a quick movement, a flurry of activity, and then a crack, or two cracks of rifle fire, and I thought, Oh, my God! I turned and started running as fast as I could. I don't think I got more than a step or two, and all of a sudden I was on the ground. It was just like somebody had come over and given me a body blow and knocked me right down.

The bullet had entered my left heel and had literally knocked me off my feet. I tried to raise myself, and I heard someone yelling, "Stay down, stay down! It's buckshot!" I looked up, and about five or ten feet away from me, behind a tree, was my roommate Alan Canfora. That was the first time I had seen him since we were down on the other side of the commons, chanting antiwar slogans.

So I threw myself back to the ground and lay as prone as possible to shield myself as much as I could, although like most people I was caught right in the open. I couldn't run, because I had already been hit. There was no cover. I just hugged the ground so as to expose as little of my body as possible to the gunfire.

It seemed like the bullets were going by within inches of my head. I can remember seeing people behind me, farther down the hill in the parking lot, dropping. I didn't know if they were being hit by bullets or they were just hugging the ground. We know today that it only lasted thirteen seconds, but it seemed like it kept going and going and going. And I remember thinking, When is this going to stop?

So I was lying there, and all of a sudden this real husky, well-built guy ran to me, picked me up like I was a sack of potatoes, and threw me over his shoulder. He carried me through the parking lot in the direction of a girls' dormitory. We went by one body, a huge puddle of blood. Head wounds always bleed very badly, and his was just awful.

The female students were screaming as I was carried into the dormitory and placed on a couch, bleeding all over the place. A nursing student applied a tourniquet to my leg. I never really felt that my life was in danger, but I could look down at my foot and I knew that I had one hell of a bad wound. The bullet blew the shoe right off my foot, and there was a bone sticking through my green sock. It looked like somebody had put my foot through a meatgrinder.

The ambulances came. Some attendants came in, put me on a stretcher, and carried me outside. The blood loss had lessened because of the tourniquet that was on my leg. I remember having my fist up in the air as a sign of defiance. They put me into the top tier in the ambulance rather than the lower one, which was already occupied. I remember my foot hitting the edge of the ambulance as I went in. From that moment on, until the time that I actually went under from the anesthesia at Robinson Memorial Hospital, I was probably in the most intense pain that I've ever experienced in my life.

They had the back doors closed by this time, and the ambulance was speeding away from the campus. I looked down and saw Sandy Scheuer. I had met Sandy about a week or two beforehand for the first and only time. She had been introduced to me by one of the guys who lived downstairs in my apartment complex. They were casual friends, and she struck me as being a very nice person.

She had a gaping bullet wound in the neck, and the ambulance attendants were tearing away the top two buttons of her blouse and then doing a heart massage. I remember their saying that it's no use, she's dead. And then they just pulled up the sheet over her head.

The ambulance got to the hospital, and it was a scene that's probably been played out any number of times when you have a big disaster. There were people running around, stretchers being wheeled in, and I was just put out in a hallway because the medical personnel were attending to the more severely wounded.

I had the tourniquet on my leg, so I wasn't bleeding all over the place, but the pain kept getting more excruciating. I was screaming by that time, "Get me something for this pain!" Then I was wheeled into an elevator and brought up to one of the other floors. I remember receiving some anesthesia and being told to count backward from ten. I didn't get very far, and then I was out.

The next thing I remember was waking up in a hospital bed. I looked up at the ceiling and then all of a sudden it came to me what had occurred. I didn't know how long I had been out, and I sat up as quickly as I could and looked down to see if my foot was still there. I could see the tips of my toes sticking out of a cast. I just lay back, and I breathed a big sigh of relief. . . .

Today, if I engage in any strenuous exercise, I'll have a noticeable limp for a couple of days afterward. But on the whole, I consider myself to be rather fortunate. I could have lost my foot; I could have been killed. Four people had been shot to death: Sandy Scheuer, Jeff Miller, Allison Krause, and Bill Schroeder. My roommate Alan Canfora was struck by gunfire. He was among the least injured of the thirteen people who were either mortally wounded or recovered.

Eventually federal indictments against enlisted men and noncommissioned officers in the Ohio National Guard were handed down. But, as it turned out, the judge ruled that the Justice Department failed to prove a case of conspiracy to violate our civil rights and dismissed the case before it was ever sent to the jury. That was the end of criminal proceedings against the Ohio National Guard. They got off scot-free.

But I think there are some guardsmen who are sorry for what happened. One guy in particular seemed to be genuinely remorseful. I remember his testimony. He has very poor eyesight, and on May 4 he couldn't get the gas mask on over his glasses, so he had to wear the gas mask without glasses. He was blind as a bat without them, and he admitted he just knew he was shooting in a certain direction. That was a startling admission. There was a guy out there who could hardly see, blasting away with an M-1. . . .

42

BELLA ABZUG

Testimony Before the New York City Human Rights Commission

September 1970

In 1970, the black feminist lawyer Eleanor Holmes Norton, chair of the New York City Human Rights Commission, organized hearings on women's rights. Bella Abzug, then running for Congress from Manhattan's West Side, described the exclusion of women from political power and prophesied a radical change. Abzug flamboyantly symbolized the resurgence of the Lefts, Old and New. In the 1950s, she had worked as a lawyer for the Civil Rights Congress, branded a "communist front organization" by the Justice Department. In the 1960s, she had been a leader of the organization Women's Strike for Peace. While in Congress, Abzug became feminism's most articulate exponent on Capitol Hill. She was also one of the first national politicians to court gay votes, visiting the Gay Activists Alliance's firehouse in lower Manhattan with great fanfare.

For most of this country's history, women have lived without visible political power, and they have been excluded from all levels of government of American society. The momentous decisions of war and peace, as well as the everyday decisions that affect how all people live, have been made by a minority of individuals who happen to be born as white males. In reality, they are still making the decisions, despite some token gestures toward representation of women and minority groups.

Nor is this exclusion of women from political power any less deliberate than exclusion of black people and other minorities. Nearly 200 years ago when our founding fathers were drawing up the Constitution of our new nation, John Adams received a letter from his wife, Abigail, which said, "My dear John, By the way, in the new code of

Reprinted in Miriam Schneir, ed., *Feminism in Our Time: The Essential Writings, World War II to the Present* (New York: Vintage, 1994), 394–98.

laws . . . I desire you would remember the ladies, and be more generous and favorable to them than your ancestors. Do not put such unlimited power in the hands of husbands. Remember all men would be tyrants if they could. Your loving wife, Abigail." Mr. Adams' reply came right to the point. "Depend upon it, my dear wife," he wrote, "we know better than to repeal our masculine systems." Just as, of course, they knew better than to repeal the system of slavery that inexorably warped the democratic development of our nation and condemned millions to misery, servitude, and repression.

So it was up to the women to repeal the "masculine systems" and it took a heartbreaking and backbreaking struggle of almost a century—a political struggle—to win the right to vote for women in 1920. In the course of that struggle, women developed and mastered every political technique that is now taken for granted in American politics—checking voting records, compiling lists by election districts, doorbell ringing, leafleting, lobbying, parading, demonstrating by the thousands, and even getting arrested.

Yes, our political skills are now very highly valued. We are allowed to do most of the drudgery and the dirty work and the detail work of politics. I would venture to say that there is no political party in the United States that could survive were it not for the fact that the women are holding up those structures on their backs. But for the most part, women are still excluded from the political power they create. Women are a majority of the population. They are also a majority in every racial and ethnic group. But they are almost invisible in government.

Out of 435 members in the House of Representatives in the Ninety-first Congress, only ten are women, including just one black woman, a great black woman, Shirley Chisholm, but just one.[1] Of course, there are no Puerto Ricans, Mexican-Americans, or Indians in Congress, women or men. Out of 100 Senators, only one is a woman and she got there initially as a replacement for her husband, who died in office.[2] There are no women on the Supreme Court, no women governors, no women mayors in big cities, and right here in New York City, Mayor [John] Lindsay confessed the other day that only a few women hold top city jobs. Some of them are good women. In Washington, as of De-

---

[1] Shirley Chisholm was elected to represent Brooklyn in Congress in 1968. Four years later, in 1972, she became the first serious woman presidential candidate in U.S. history, running a creditable race in the Democratic primaries.

[2] The one female senator in 1970, and for many decades before, was Republican Margaret Chase Smith from Maine.

cember 1969, of more than 300 administration posts filled by President Nixon, only thirteen have gone to women, and three of those are White House secretaries.

This is merely one aspect of the discrimination against women that blights all parts of our society—economically, legally, and socially, as well as politically. But in this year of women's liberation movements, in this year when passage of the Equal Rights Amendment has finally come within sight, women are speaking up more militantly than ever for equality, and they are determined—and we shall get what is our due. . . .

There is one thing women can change—and that is the Congress of the United States and the political power structure of our country. And we are not going to wait another fifty years to do so. If some men complain that we are "boisterous and aggressive" instead of "delightful and delectable" . . . that's all right with us. We cannot all be Shirley Temples, nor do we want to be.

Women are going to set political goals of full representation in government, not just tokenism. Within the next few years—let us say by the 200th birthday of our nation's founding—women must fight for and win a political structure that mirrors reality. And along the way, they will find many allies among men and political organizations who recognize that a society which, at long last, gives full scope to the abilities and creativity of half its population can only gain in health, wisdom, and strength. . . .

Suppose, for example, that instead of just eleven women in the House and Senate, we had several hundred—and I am not talking about just middle-class professional women, but about representatives of America's 30 million working women, women from the garment factories of midtown Manhattan, the auto plants of Detroit, from the great vineyards of California and the cotton fields of the South, from laundries, schools, and hospitals, and women who work at home—shopping, cooking, cleaning, raising kids, and performing the hundreds of thousands of volunteer jobs that keep our society functioning.

Needless to say, such a Congress would not tolerate the countless laws on the books that discriminate against women in all phases of their lives. But more than that. Does anyone think that with that kind of representation we would have reached the twilight of the twentieth century without a national health care system for all Americans? Would we rank fourteenth in infant mortality among the developed nations of the world? Would we allow a situation in which thousands of kids grow up without decent care because their mothers have to work for a living and have no place to leave their children, or else that condemns women to stay at home when they want to work, because there are no facilities for their children? Would a Congress with large numbers of women condone the continued murdering of young girls and mothers in amateur abortion mills, or would it guarantee that the right to free abortions belonged in all parts of the country? Would women allow the fraudulent packaging and cheating of consumers that they find every time they shop? Would they consent to the perverted sense of priorities that has dominated our government for the past few decades, appropriating billions of dollars for war and plunging our cities into crises of neglect? Would they vote for ABMs instead of schools, MIRVs instead of decent housing or health centers?[3] And does anyone think they would have allowed the war in Vietnam to go on for so many years, slaughtering and maiming our young men and the people of Indochina?

This may all sound like wishful thinking: the thought that someday we may have a Fannie Lou Hamer instead of a James Eastland in the Senate may seem too absurd.[4] Indeed, even the suggestion that we should have ten or twenty times as many women in Congress as we now have, or that there should be women on the Supreme Court, or in the White House, will no doubt provoke haughty editorial lectures about exaggerated demands, or psychological tomes about the castration complexes of women or, at the very least, keep the gag writers for *Laugh-In* busy for weeks.[5]

But I suggest that what is really ludicrous is a political structure that denies representation to a majority of its population and then winds up fingering the victims of this situation as somehow responsible for it because of their personal inadequacies.

This is the same historic game of one-upmanship that is being so magnificently rejected by black Americans, and women now are recognizing that they too will have to join in militant action for their rights. I am not going to lecture women about the responsibilities of citizenship, or the need to get out and vote—but do it anyhow—or to join political movements. Women are *in* politics. They know *how* to

---

[3] ABMS (antiballistic missiles) and MIRVS (multiple independently targeted reentry vehicles, or multiheaded guided missiles) were two new, extremely costly weapons systems proposed by President Nixon and supported by a majority in Congress.

[4] Civil rights activist Fannie Lou Hamer and segregationist senator James Eastland both came from Sunflower County, Mississippi.

[5] *Laugh-In* was an extremely popular comedy-variety show in the late 1960s and early 1970s.

organize. They recognize their needs. But they are going to have to upgrade their demands and seek a full share in political power and leadership. And I submit that what is good for women will turn out to be good for the entire country.

43

JOHN KERRY

Vietnam Veterans Against the War Testimony to the U.S. Senate Foreign Relations Committee

April 22, 1971

Vietnam Veterans Against the War (VVAW) was founded in 1967. Part of a growing antiwar movement within the military spurred by hundreds of "GI coffeehouses" run by local antiwar civilians, VVAW sought to use the authority of its members as combat veterans to expose the brutality and immorality of the war. The group's "limited incursion" into Washington, D.C., in April 1971 (a phrase mocking President Nixon's description of his invasion of Cambodia) was a high point of the antiwar movement. Wearing their old uniforms, the veterans, many in wheelchairs, camped illegally on the Capitol grounds. VVAW leader John Kerry testified before the Senate Foreign Relations Committee. His famous question—"How do you ask a man to be the last man to die for a mistake?"—has never been effectively answered.

Thank you very much, Senator Fulbright, Senator Javits, Senator Symington, Senator Pell. I would like to say for the record, and also for the men behind me who are also wearing the uniform and their medals, that my sitting here is really symbolic. I am not here as John Kerry. I am here as one member of the group of 1,000 which is a small representation of a very much larger group of veterans in this

Reprinted in Marvin E. Gettleman, Jane Franklin, Marilyn B. Young, and H. Bruce Franklin, eds., *Vietnam and America: A Documented History,* 2nd ed. (New York: Grove Press, 1995), 456–62.

country, and were it possible for all of them to sit at this table they would be here and have the same kind of testimony. . . .

I would like to talk on behalf of all those veterans and say that several months ago in Detroit we had an investigation at which over 150 honorably discharged, and many very highly decorated, veterans testified to war crimes committed in Southeast Asia. These were not isolated incidents but crimes committed on a day to day basis with the full awareness of officers at all levels of command.

It is impossible to describe to you exactly what did happen in Detroit—the emotions in the room and the feelings of the men who were reliving their experiences in Vietnam. They relived the absolute horror of what this country, in a sense, made them do.

They told stories that at times they had personally raped, cut off ears, cut off heads, taped wires from portable telephones to human genitals and turned up the power, cut off limbs, blown up bodies, randomly shot at civilians, razed villages in fashion reminiscent of Genghis Khan, shot cattle and dogs for fun, poisoned food stocks, and generally ravaged the countryside of South Vietnam in addition to the normal ravage of war and the normal and very particular ravaging which is done by the applied bombing power of this country.

We call this investigation the Winter Soldier Investigation. The term Winter Soldier is a play on words of Thomas Paine's in 1776 when he spoke of the Sunshine Patriots and summer time soldiers who deserted at Valley Forge because the going was rough.

We who have come here to Washington have come here because we feel we have to be winter soldiers now. We could come back to this country, we could be quiet, we could hold our silence, we could not tell what went on in Vietnam, but we feel because of what threatens this country, not the reds, but the crimes which we are committing that threaten it, that we have to speak out.

I would like to talk to you a little bit about what the result is of the feelings these men carry with them after coming back from Vietnam. The country doesn't know it yet but it has created a monster, a monster in the form of millions of men who have been taught to deal and to trade in violence and who are given the chance to die for the biggest nothing in history; men who have returned with a sense of anger and a sense of betrayal which no one has yet grasped.

As a veteran and one who feels this anger I would like to talk about it. We are angry because we feel we have been used in the worst fashion by the administration of this country.

In 1970 at West Point Vice President Agnew said "some glamorize the criminal misfits of society while our best men die in Asian rice paddies to preserve the freedom which most of those misfits abuse," and this was used as a rallying point for our effort in Vietnam.

But for us, as boys in Asia whom the country was supposed to support, his statement is a terrible distortion from which we can only draw a very deep sense of revulsion, and hence the anger of some of the men who are here in Washington today. It is a distortion because we in no way consider ourselves the best men of this country; because those he calls misfits were standing up for us in a way that nobody else in this country dared to; because so many who have died would have returned to this country to join the misfits in their efforts to ask for an immediate withdrawal from South Vietnam; because so many of those best men have returned as quadriplegics and amputees—and they lie forgotten in Veterans Administration Hospitals in this country which fly the flag which so many have chosen as their own personal symbol—and we cannot consider ourselves America's best men when we are ashamed of and hated for what we were called on to do in Southeast Asia.

In our opinion, and from our experience, there is nothing in South Vietnam which could happen that realistically threatens the United States of America. And to attempt to justify the loss of one American life in Vietnam, Cambodia or Laos by linking such loss to the preservation of freedom, which those misfits supposedly abuse, is to us the height of criminal hypocrisy, and it is that kind of hypocrisy which we feel has torn this country apart.

We are probably much more angry than that, but I don't want to go into the foreign policy aspects because I am outclassed here. I know that all of you talk about every possible alternative for getting out of Vietnam. We understand that. We know you have considered the seriousness of the aspects to the utmost level and I am not going to try to dwell on that. But I want to relate to you the feeling that many of the men who have returned to this country express because we are probably angriest about all that we were told about Vietnam and about the mystical war against communism.

We found that not only was it a civil war, an effort by a people who had for years been seeking their liberation from any colonial influence whatsoever, but also we found that the Vietnamese whom we had enthusiastically molded after our own image were hard put to take up the fight against the threat we were supposedly saving them from.

We found most people didn't even know the difference between communism and democracy. They only wanted to work in rice paddies without helicopters strafing them and bombs with napalm burning their villages and tearing their country apart. They wanted everything to do with the war, particularly with this foreign presence of the United States of America, to leave them alone in peace, and they practiced the art of survival by siding with whichever military force was present at a particular time, be it Viet Cong, North Vietnamese or American.

We found also that all too often American men were dying in those rice paddies for want of support from their allies. We saw first hand how monies from American taxes were used for a corrupt dictatorial regime. We saw that many people in this country had a one-sided idea of who was kept free by our flag, and blacks provided the highest percentage of casualties. We saw Vietnam ravaged equally by American bombs and search and destroy missions, as well as by Viet Cong terrorism, and yet we listened while this country tried to blame all of the havoc on the Viet Cong.

We rationalized destroying villages in order to save them. We saw America lose her sense of morality as she accepted very coolly a My Lai[1] and refused to give up the image of American soldiers who hand out chocolate bars and chewing gum.

We learned the meaning of free fire zones, shooting anything that moves, and we watched while America placed a cheapness on the lives of orientals.

We watched the United States falsification of body counts, in fact the glorification of body counts. We listened while month after month we were told the back of the enemy was about to break. We fought using weapons against "oriental human beings." We fought using weapons against those people which I do not believe this country would dream of using were we fighting in the European theater. We watched while men charged up hills because a general said that hill has to be taken, and after losing one platoon or two platoons they marched away to leave the hill for reoccupation by the North Vietnamese. We watched pride allow the most unimportant battles to be blown into extravaganzas, because we couldn't lose, and we couldn't retreat, and because it didn't matter how many American bodies were lost to prove that point, and so there were Hamburger Hills and Khe Sanhs and Hill 81s and Fire Base 6s, and so many others.[2]

---

[1]My Lai was the site of a notorious war crime in Vietnam in March 1968, where a U.S. Army company led by Lieutenant William Calley massacred several hundred Vietnamese women, children, and old people. Knowledge of the massacre only became public in late 1969.

[2]These are the names of famous battles in the Vietnam War, all of which ended as bloody stalemates.

Now we are told that the men who fought there must watch quietly while American lives are lost so that we can exercise the incredible arrogance of Vietnamizing the Vietnamese.

Each day to facilitate the process by which the United States washes her hands of Vietnam someone has to give up his life so that the United States doesn't have to admit something that the entire world already knows, so that we can't say that we have made a mistake. Someone has to die so that President Nixon won't be, and these are his words, "the first President to lose a war."

We are asking Americans to think about that because how do you ask a man to be the last man to die in Vietnam? How do you ask a man to be the last man to die for a mistake? But we are trying to do that, and we are doing it with thousands of rationalizations, and if you read carefully the President's last speech to the people of this country, you can see that he says, and says clearly, "but the issue, gentlemen, is communism, and the question is whether or not we will leave that country to the communists or whether or not we will try to give it hope to be a free people." But the point is they are not a free people now under us. They are not a free people, and we cannot fight communism all over the world. I think we should have learned that lesson by now. . . .

Finally, this administration has done us the ultimate dishonor. They have attempted to disown us and the sacrifices we made for this country. In their blindness and fear they have tried to deny that we are veterans or that we served in Nam. We do not need their testimony. Our own scars and stumps of limbs are witness enough for others and for ourselves.

We wish that a merciful God could wipe away our own memories of that service as easily as this administration has wiped away their memories of us. But all that they have done and all that they can do by this denial is to make more clear than ever our own determination to undertake one last mission—to search out and destroy the last vestige of this barbaric war, to pacify our own hearts, to conquer the hate and the fear that have driven this country these last ten years and more, so when 30 years from now our brothers go down the street without a leg, without an arm, or a face, and small boys ask why, we will be able to say "Vietnam" and not mean a desert, not a filthy obscene memory, but mean instead the place where America finally turned and where soldiers like us helped it in the turning.

Thank you.

44

CHARLES DIGGS JR.

Speech at the Congressional Black Caucus Dinner
June 18, 1971

A tangible measure of Black Power was a sweeping increase in African Americans being elected to office. Until the late 1960s, their numbers were minuscule. The Congressional Black Caucus (CBC) founded in January 1971, held its first annual dinner in June of that year. Representative Charles Diggs Jr. of Detroit, chair of the caucus, gave the keynote address. Diggs was first elected to Congress in 1954, becoming one of only three black congressmen. He was an outspoken supporter of civil rights and saw the CBC as a way to establish the political independence of African Americans. In the 1970s Diggs frequently traveled to Africa, negotiated with leaders there on behalf of the CBC, and intervened in U.S. diplomacy in favor of African interests—all unprecedented actions for an African American politician. His speech set the militant tone that the CBC has maintained since then as the bastion of the Democratic Party's left wing.

I welcome you on behalf of the thirteen members of the Congressional Black Caucus. But we welcome you, too, on behalf of our colleagues from cities and states all over the nation who have done us the honor of joining us here, and of the millions not physically present tonight who have over the past several years mounted a quiet revolution through their ballots—a revolution which is changing both the direction—and the complexion—of municipal, county, and state governments north, south, east, and west.

We meet tonight in the majority-black capital of this most powerful nation in the world which somehow seems powerless to solve its most fundamental problems. We meet to assert the common bonds that unite men and women of all races, creeds, and generations who share a fierce determination to liberate the legions of the oppressed. We come together to arm and equip ourselves to fight more effectively

Reprinted in William L. Clay, *Just Permanent Interests: Black Americans in Congress, 1870–1991* (New York: Amistad, 1992), 164–65.

than ever before for those who are too seldom victors, too often victims. The victims of poverty and racism, of a senseless war, of an economy which offers neither enough jobs nor the dignity of an adequate income. The victims of that contemporary plague, drug addiction, which is now visiting upon our soldiers and the citizens of the suburbs the same human destruction to which our country paid little heed when the casualties were largely confined to the black and brown youth of our urban ghettos.

The response which your generous outpouring of aid and encouragement tonight represents, reflects the range and depth of support which the Caucus has had the rare good fortune to receive since its inception.

. . . With the staff and resources we plan to assemble after tonight, we hope to be clearer, more persistent, and more effective than blacks in the national Congress have ever been in fashioning an agenda not only for 1972, but for years to come.

. . . As it happens, all of us are Democrats. But what we are hearing with increasing insistence from our constituents is that there are times when they would have us judge our interests by something more substantial than party labels. And there are likely to be times when we must challenge both major parties and candidates of every persuasion, at every level, to address forthrightly the unmet needs of our people.

. . . Even as we celebrate, even as we enjoy the wit, beauty, and soul of some of the most gifted artists in America, let us not forget that it is by no easy path that we have arrived at this night. And the journey is far from over. We are the grateful heirs of Douglass, Du Bois, and Bethune—of Medgar Evers, Malcolm, Martin Luther King, and Whitney Young. We build on the labors of Thurgood Marshall, Adam Clayton Powell, Roy Wilkins, the young men and women of the civil rights movement of the sixties, and the black thrust toward long-denied power and liberation which is part of the worldwide revolution of color and the rejection of caste. . . .[1]

---

[1] Besides Malcolm X and Martin Luther King Jr., Diggs named a pantheon of important African American activists from across the ideological spectrum: the nineteenth-century abolitionist Frederick Douglass; W. E. B. Du Bois, cofounder of the NAACP; Mary McLeod Bethune, a leading educator and government official under Franklin Roosevelt; Medgar Evers, the NAACP field secretary assassinated in Mississippi in 1963; Whitney Young, head of the Urban League, a moderate civil rights group; Thurgood Marshall, the NAACP lawyer who litigated *Brown v. Board of Education* in the early 1950s and became the first African American named to the U.S. Supreme Court in 1967; Adam Clayton Powell, congressman from Harlem, 1945–67 and 1969–71; and Roy Wilkins, longtime NAACP head.

45

BOSTON WOMEN'S HEALTH BOOK COLLECTIVE

Our Bodies, Ourselves

1973

Our Bodies, Ourselves *is a remarkable example of what one feminist "small group" could achieve. A consciousness-raising discussion among a few women at a 1969 conference revealed a shared frustration with the medical profession. On their own, this group, the Boston Women's Health Book Collective, developed a free workshop and a series of pamphlets about women's health — birth control, childbirth, menstruation, the mechanics of reproductive organs, and more. Turned into a newsprint book by the radical New England Free Press, it sold 250,000 copies (ten cents each when sold in bulk) from 1970 to 1973. Simon and Schuster, a mainstream publisher, bought the rights to the book in 1973. Regularly updated, it has sold more than three million copies over the past thirty years. The Boston Women's Health Book Collective's share of the book's profits is used to fund women's health projects.*

The history of this book, *Our Bodies, Ourselves,* is lengthy and satisfying.

It began at a small discussion group on "women and their bodies" which was part of a women's conference held in Boston in the spring of 1969. These were the early days of the women's movement, one of the first gatherings of women meeting specifically to talk with other women. For many of us it was the very first time we got together with other women to talk and think about our lives and what we could do about them. Before the conference was over some of us decided to keep on meeting as a group to continue the discussion, and so we did.

In the beginning we called the group "the doctor's group." We had all experienced similar feelings of frustration and anger toward specific doctors and the medical maze in general, and initially we wanted to do something about those doctors who were condescending, paternalistic, judgmental, and non-informative. As we talked and shared our

---

Reprinted in Miriam Schneir, ed., *Feminism in Our Time: The Essential Writings, World War II to the Present* (New York: Vintage, 1994), 353–60.

experiences with one another, we realized just how much we had to learn about our bodies. So we decided on a summer project—to research those topics which we felt were particularly pertinent to learning about our bodies, to discuss in the group what we had learned, then to write papers individually or in small groups of two or three, and finally to present the results in the fall as a course for women on women and their bodies.

As we developed the course we realized more and more that we were really capable of collecting, understanding, and evaluating medical information. Together we evaluated our reading of books and journals, our talks with doctors and friends who were medical students. We found we could discuss, question, and argue with each other in a new spirit of cooperation rather than competition. We were equally struck by how important it was for us to be able to open up with one another and share our feelings about our bodies. The process of talking was as crucial as the facts themselves. Over time the facts and feelings melted together in ways that touched us very deeply, and that is reflected in the changing titles of the course and then the book— from *Women and Their Bodies* to *Women and Our Bodies* to, finally, *Our Bodies, Ourselves.*

When we gave the course we met in any available free space we could get—in day schools, in nursery schools, in churches, in our homes. We expected the course to stimulate the same kind of talking and sharing that we who had prepared the course had experienced. We had something to say, but we had a lot to learn as well; we did not want a traditional teacher-student relationship. At the end of ten to twelve sessions—which roughly covered the material in the current book—we found that many women felt both eager and competent to get together in small groups and share what they had learned with other women. We saw it as a never-ending process always involving more and more women.

After the first teaching of the course, we decided to revise our initial papers and mimeograph them so that other women could have copies as the course expanded. Eventually we got them printed and bound together in an inexpensive edition published by the New England Free Press. It was fascinating and very exciting for us to see what a constant demand there was for our book. It came out in several editions, a larger number being printed each time, and the time from one printing to the next becoming shorter. The growing volume of requests began to strain the staff of the New England Free Press. Since our book was clearly speaking to many people, we wanted to reach beyond the audience who lived in the area or who were acquainted with the New England Free Press. For wider distribution it made sense to publish our book commercially.

You may want to know who we are. Our ages range from twenty-five to forty-one, most of us are from middle-class backgrounds and have had at least some college education, and some of us have professional degrees. Some of us are married, some of us are separated, and some of us are single. Some of us have children of our own, some of us like spending time with children, and others of us are not sure we want to be with children. In short, we are both a very ordinary and a very special group, as women are everywhere. We are white middle-class women, and as such can describe only what life has been for us. But we do realize that poor women and non-white women have suffered far more from the kinds of misinformation and mistreatment that we are describing in this book. In some ways, learning about our womanhood from the inside out has allowed us to cross over the socially created barriers of race, color, income, and class, and to feel a sense of identity with all women in the experience of being female.

We are eleven individuals and we are a group. (The group has been ongoing for three years and some of us have been together since the beginning. Others came in at later points. Our current collective has been together for one year.) We know each other well—our weaknesses as well as our strengths. We have learned through good times and bad how to work together (and how not to as well). We recognize our similarities and differences and are learning to respect each person for her uniqueness. We love each other. . . .

A Chronology of Key Events
in the History of the New Left
(1949–1975)

1949 Under the Alien Registration Act of 1940, also called the Smith Act, Communist Party leaders are convicted of conspiring to advocate the overthrow of the U.S. government by force; Communist-led unions are expelled from the Congress of Industrial Organizations (CIO).

1950 Mattachine Society is founded in Los Angeles to advocate for homosexual rights.

1954

May U.S. Supreme Court declares school segregation unconstitutional in *Brown v. Board of Education;* in response, southern whites form Citizens Councils to lead a campaign of "massive resistance" to desegregation.

1955

December Bus boycott begins in Montgomery, Alabama; the Reverend Martin Luther King Jr. is drafted as spokesman.

1956

March Liberation magazine begins publication.

1957

January U.S. Supreme Court overturns Montgomery's bus segregation law; King forms the Southern Christian Leadership Conference (SCLC).

September President Dwight Eisenhower sends troops to Little Rock, Arkansas, to enforce desegregation and protect African American children entering a white high school.

November Committee for a Sane Nuclear Policy (SANE) is founded.

1959

January Fidel Castro's 26th of July Revolutionary Movement overthrows U.S.-backed president Fulgencio Batista in Cuba.

1960

February Black students "sit in" at a lunch counter in Greensboro, North Carolina, sparking civil disobedience across the South.

April Sit-in leaders create the Student Nonviolent Coordinating Committee (SNCC); Fair Play for Cuba Committee (FPCC) is founded.

November Kennedy defeats Nixon for the presidency.

1961

April Bay of Pigs invasion fails amid nationwide protests.

May Congress of Racial Equality (CORE) sends integrated teams of Freedom Riders into the Deep South.

November Women's Strike for Peace organizes a nationwide mothers' protest against nuclear war.

1962

June Students for a Democratic Society (SDS) issues *The Port Huron Statement.*

October White mobs attack U.S. marshals sent to enforce desegregation at the University of Mississippi.

October–November Cuban missile crisis occurs.

1963

February Betty Friedan's *The Feminine Mystique* is published.

April SCLC targets Birmingham, Alabama, for a civil rights campaign.

June Kennedy calls for "peaceful revolution" in the South; Medgar Evers is assassinated.

August March for Jobs and Freedom takes place in Washington, D.C.

August–September Kennedy signs the Limited Test Ban Treaty with the Soviet Union and convinces the Senate to pass it.

September Ku Klux Klan bombs a Birmingham church, killing four African American girls.

November Kennedy is assassinated in Dallas; Lyndon Johnson becomes president.

1964

March Malcolm X leaves the Nation of Islam and forms the Organization of Afro-American Unity.

June Freedom Summer Project brings northern students to Mississippi.

July Civil Rights Act outlaws discrimination based on race, ethnicity, religion, and sex.

August Mississippi Freedom Democratic Party (MFDP) refuses a compromise at the Democratic National Convention.

October Free Speech Movement (FSM) begins at the University of California at Berkeley.

November Johnson wins a sweeping victory over Republican Barry Goldwater.

December King wins the Nobel Peace Prize.

1965

February Malcolm X is assassinated in Harlem.

March Civil rights marchers are beaten in Selma, Alabama; Johnson pressures Congress to pass a voting rights act; U.S. Marines land in Vietnam, beginning a massive buildup of ground troops; "teach-in" on Vietnam at the University of Michigan spreads nationwide.

April SDS leads a march against the Vietnam War in Washington, D.C.

August Watts uprising breaks out in Los Angeles.

November First large-scale draft card burnings occur in New York.

1966

June During a civil rights march in Mississippi, SNCC's Stokely Carmichael calls for "Black Power."

October National Organization for Women (NOW) is founded; Black Panther Party for Self-Defense (BPP) is organized in Oakland.

December Chicago conference creates the Resistance, an antidraft network.

1967

April During the Spring Mobilization against the War, 200,000 rally in New York and 50,000 in San Francisco.

Summer Black urban rebellions paralyze Detroit and Newark, New Jersey.

October One hundred thousand protesters surround the Pentagon to demand an end to the war in Vietnam.

November Senator Eugene McCarthy announces his antiwar presidential candidacy; Carl Stokes is elected mayor of Cleveland, becoming the first African American mayor of a major city.

1968

January Tet Offensive by South Vietnam's National Liberation Front (Vietcong).

February McCarthy almost beats Johnson in the New Hampshire Democratic primary.

March Johnson withdraws from the presidential race and announces a halt to the bombing in Vietnam and the beginning of peace negotiations; "blowouts" by Chicano youths occur in Los Angeles high schools.

April King is assassinated in Memphis, and 109 cities erupt in violence; student strike occurs at Columbia University.

May Berrigan brothers lead a raid on the draft board in Catonsville, Maryland.

August "Police riot" occurs at the Democratic National Convention in Chicago; Vice President Hubert Humphrey is nominated.

September Miss America pageant protest is staged by New York Radical Women (NYRW).

November Nixon narrowly defeats Humphrey; segregationist George Wallace runs third.

1969

April Chicano student leaders in California form Movimiento Estudiantil Chicano de Aztlán (MEChA).

June When SDS collapses, one faction forms Weatherman; gay men confront police after a raid on the Stonewall Inn in New York's Greenwich Village.

July Gay Liberation Front (GLF) is founded; Young Lords Party (YLP) is founded in New York's East Harlem.

October Millions participate in the Moratorium against the war.

November In the largest antiwar rally to date, 500,000 march on Washington, D.C.; Native American activists occupy the former federal prison on Alcatraz Island in San Francisco Bay.

December Gay Activists Alliance (GAA) is founded in New York.

1970

January Women's Equity Action League files a class action lawsuit against every university in the United States for sex discrimination.

April–May Nixon orders the invasion of Cambodia; nationwide student strike begins; four students are killed at Kent State in Ohio, two at Jackson State in Mississippi.

May "Lavender Menace" disrupts NOW's Second Congress to Unite Women.

August NOW leads Women's Strike for Equality demonstrations nationwide.

1971

January Congressional Black Caucus (CBC) is established.

April Vietnam Veterans Against the War (VVAW) organizes a return of members' medals at the U.S. Capitol during the last major antiwar rally.

July National Women's Political Caucus is created by Betty Friedan, Gloria Steinem, Representatives Bella Abzug and Shirley Chisholm, and others.

1972

March National Black Political Assembly is held in Gary, Indiana; Senate approves the Equal Rights Amendment (ERA; approved by House in 1971) and sends it to the states for ratification.

July First issue of *Ms.* magazine sells out.

August Antiwar Senator George McGovern of South Dakota wins the Democratic presidential nomination.

November Nixon defeats McGovern, winning 61 percent of the vote.

1973

January United States signs the final peace accord with North Vietnam; U.S. Supreme Court's *Roe v. Wade* decision legalizes abortion.

February American Indian Movement (AIM) leads an armed occupation of Wounded Knee on the Pine Ridge Reservation in South Dakota.

August Congress cuts off all funding for the air war in Southeast Asia.

November Coleman Young, an African American, is elected mayor of Detroit, America's fifth-largest city.

December American Psychiatric Association removes its classification of homosexuality as a mental illness.

1974

August Nixon resigns the presidency and is pardoned by President Gerald Ford.

1975

April South Vietnamese government and army collapse; Saigon falls, and Vietnam is reunited; war ends.

Questions for Consideration

1. What was cold war liberalism? How did the movements of the New Left relate to mainstream liberalism before the Vietnam War escalated in 1965?

2. What common strategies and tactics were used by the different movements? How did they inspire and learn from one another? Were particular types of protest used by all the movements?

3. Why was the civil rights movement the driving force of the New Left in 1955–65? What were the major groups in that movement? What role did Martin Luther King Jr. play?

4. Why was the Cuban Revolution important to various movements of the early New Left?

5. What was the connection between the 1964 Mississippi Freedom Summer Project and the Free Speech Movement at Berkeley? Why did white students in groups such as Students for a Democratic Society (SDS) rebel, and what did they rebel against?

6. What led to the revival of feminism in the 1960s? What various groups of women made it possible? What did they have in common?

7. What did Black Power and the civil rights movement have in common? How did they differ? Why did some civil rights activists embrace Black Power?

8. How did the Vietnam War change the relationship between the New Left and cold war liberals such as Lyndon Johnson? What were the different groups and trends in the antiwar movement?

9. How did the events of 1968 shift the political terrain for the New Left movements?

10. After 1968, why did significant numbers of liberals become radicalized? What happened to the Democratic Party from 1968 to 1972 and after?

11. How was the women's liberation movement organized? What made it different from the other movements?

12. What did the African American, Native American, Chicano, Puerto Rican, and Asian American movements have in common? How did they differ? Why did so many of these movements appear at the same time?

13. What were the differences between the homophile movement of the 1950s and 1960s and the gay liberation movement after the Stonewall riot in 1969?

14. What happened to the individual movements of the New Left in the 1970s? Did the New Left die, or is it still part of our political and cultural lives today?

15. How did the New Left contribute to the rise of the New Right?

Selected Bibliography

IMPORTANT EARLY STUDIES

Essien-Udom, Essien. *Black Nationalism: A Search for Identity in America.* Chicago: University of Chicago Press, 1962.

Jacobs, Paul, and Saul Landau. *The New Radicals: A Report with Documents.* New York: Vintage, 1966.

Newfield, Jack. *A Prophetic Minority.* New York: New American Library, 1966.

Oglesby, Carl. *The New Left Reader.* New York: Grove, 1969.

Sale, Kirkpatrick. *SDS.* New York: Random House, 1973.

Teal, Donn. *The Gay Militants: How Gay Liberation Began in America, 1969–1971.* New York: Stein and Day, 1971; repr., New York: St. Martin's Press, 1995.

Teodori, Massimo, ed. *The New Left: A Documentary History.* Indianapolis: Bobbs Merrill, 1969.

Zinn, Howard. *SNCC: The New Abolitionists.* Boston: Beacon Press, 1965.

GENERAL HISTORIES AND HISTORIOGRAPHY OF THE NEW LEFT
AND THE SIXTIES

Farber, David R. *The Age of Great Dreams: America in the 1960s.* New York: Hill and Wang, 1994.

Fink, Carole, Phillip Gassert, and Detlef Junker. *1968: The World Transformed.* Cambridge: Cambridge University Press, 1998.

Gitlin, Todd. *The Sixties: Years of Hope, Days of Rage.* New York: Bantam Books, 1987.

———. *The Whole World Is Watching: Mass Media in the Making and Unmaking of the New Left.* Berkeley: University of California Press, 1980.

Gosse, Van. "A Movement of Movements: The Definition and Periodization of the New Left." In *A Companion to Post-1945 America,* ed. Roy Rosenzweig and Jean-Christophe Agnew. London: Blackwell, 2002.

Isserman, Maurice. *If I Had a Hammer: The Death of the Old Left and the Birth of the New Left.* New York: Basic Books, 1987.

183

Isserman, Maurice, and Michael Kazin. *America Divided: The Civil War of the 1960s.* New York: Oxford University Press, 2000.

Katsiaficas, George. *The Imagination of the New Left: A Global Analysis of 1968.* Boston: South End Press, 1987.

Marwick, Arthur. *The Sixties: Cultural Revolution in Britain, France, Italy, and the United States, c. 1958–c. 1974.* New York: Oxford University Press, 1998.

Monhollon, Rusty. *This Is America? The Sixties in Lawrence, Kansas.* New York: Palgrave, 2002.

Sayres, Sohnya, Anders Stephanson, Stanley Aronowitz, and Frederick Jameson. *The Sixties, without Apology.* Minneapolis: University of Minnesota Press, 1984.

THE BLACK FREEDOM MOVEMENT: CIVIL RIGHTS AND BLACK POWER

Biondi, Martha. *To Stand and Fight: The Struggle for Civil Rights in Postwar New York City.* Cambridge, Mass.: Harvard University Press, 2003.

Carson, Clayborne. *In Struggle: SNCC and the Black Awakening of the 1960s.* Cambridge, Mass.: Harvard University Press, 1981.

Chafe, William H. *Civilities and Civil Rights: Greensboro, North Carolina, and the Black Struggle for Freedom.* New York: Oxford University Press, 1980.

Churchill, Ward, and Jim Vander Wall. *Agents of Repression: The FBI's Secret Wars against the Black Panther Party and the American Indian Movement.* Boston: South End Press, 1988.

Cummins, Eric. *The Rise and Fall of California's Radical Prison Movement.* Stanford, Calif.: Stanford University Press, 1994.

Dittmer, John. *Local People: The Struggle for Civil Rights in Mississippi.* Urbana: University of Illinois Press, 1994.

Georgakas, Dan, and Marvin Surkin. *Detroit: I Do Mind Dying, A Study in Urban Revolution.* New York: St. Martin's Press, 1975.

Jones, Charles E. *The Black Panther Party Reconsidered.* Baltimore: Black Classic Press, 1998.

Lawson, Steven. *Black Ballots: Voting Rights in the South, 1944–1969.* Lanham, Md.: Lexington, 1999.

———. "Freedom Then, Freedom Now: The Historiography of the Civil Rights Movement," *American Historical Review,* 96 (1991): 456–71.

———. *Running for Freedom: Civil Rights and Black Politics in America since 1941.* New York: McGraw-Hill, 1997.

Marable, Manning. *Black American Politics: From the Washington Marches to Jesse Jackson.* London: Verso, 1985.

———. *Race, Reform and Rebellion: The Second Reconstruction in Black America, 1945–1990.* Jackson: University of Mississippi Press, 1991.

Meier, August, and Elliott Rudwick. *CORE: A Study of the Civil Rights Movement, 1942–1968.* Urbana: University of Illinois Press, 1975.

Morris, Aldon D. *The Origins of the Civil Rights Movement: Black Communities Organizing for Change.* New York: Free Press, 1984.

Norrell, Robert. *Reaping the Whirlwind: The Civil Rights Movement in Tuskegee.* New York: Alfred A. Knopf, 1985.

Payne, Charles M. *I've Got the Light of Freedom: The Organizing Tradition and the Mississippi Freedom Struggle.* Berkeley: University of California Press, 1995.

Self, Robert. *American Babylon: Race and the Struggle for Postwar Oakland.* Princeton, N.J.: Princeton University Press, 2003.

Sitkoff, Harvard. *The Struggle for Black Equality, 1954–1992.* New York: Hill and Wang, 1993.

Smith, Suzanne E. *Dancing in the Street: Motown and the Cultural Politics of Detroit.* Cambridge, Mass.: Harvard University Press, 1999.

Van DeBurg, William L. *New Day in Babylon: The Black Power Movement and American Culture, 1965–1975.* Chicago: University of Chicago Press, 1992.

THE STUDENT NEW LEFT

Breines, Wini. *Community and Organization in the New Left, 1962–1968: The Great Refusal.* New Brunswick, N.J.: Rutgers University Press, 1989.

Elbaum, Max. *Revolution in the Air: Sixties Radicals Turn to Lenin, Mao, and Che.* New York: Verso, 2002.

Fraser, Ronald, et al. *1968: A Student Generation in Revolt.* New York: Pantheon, 1988.

Jacobs, Ron. *The Way the Wind Blew: A History of the Weather Underground.* London: Verso, 1997.

Miller, James. *"Democracy Is in the Streets": From Port Huron to the Siege of Chicago.* New York: Simon and Schuster, 1987.

Rorabaugh, W. J. *Berkeley at War: The 1960s.* New York: Oxford University Press, 1989.

Rossinow, Douglas. *The Politics of Authenticity: Liberalism, Christianity, and the New Left in America.* New York: Columbia University Press, 1998.

PEACE AND ANTIWAR ORGANIZING

DeBenedetti, Charles, with Charles Chatfield. *An American Ordeal: The Antiwar Movement of the Vietnam Era.* Syracuse, N.Y.: Syracuse University Press, 1990.

Farber, David R. *Chicago '68.* Chicago: University of Chicago Press, 1988.

Fisher, James Terence. *The Catholic Counterculture in America, 1933–1962.* Chapel Hill: University of North Carolina Press, 1989.

Gosse, Van. *Where the Boys Are: Cuba, Cold War America and the Making of a New Left.* London: Verso, 1993.

Hall, Mitchell K. *Because of Their Faith: CALCAV and Religious Opposition to the Vietnam War.* New York: Columbia University Press, 1990.

Heineman, Kenneth J. *Campus Wars: The Peace Movement at American State Universities in the Vietnam Era.* New York: New York University Press, 1993.

Hunt, Andrew E. *The Turning: A History of Vietnam Veterans Against the War.* New York: New York University Press, 1999.

Katz, Milton S. *Ban the Bomb: A History of SANE, the Committee for a Sane Nuclear Policy.* New York: Praeger, 1987.

Meconis, Charles. *With Clumsy Grace: The American Catholic Left, 1961–1975.* New York: Seabury Press, 1979.

Moser, Richard. *The New Winter Soldiers: GI and Veteran Dissent during the Vietnam Era.* New Brunswick, N.J.: Rutgers University Press, 1996.

Swerdlow, Amy. *Women Strike for Peace: Traditional Motherhood and Radical Politics in the 1960s.* Chicago: University of Chicago Press, 1993.

Wittner, Lawrence. *The Struggle against the Bomb: Resisting the Bomb — A History of the World Nuclear Disarmament Movement, 1954–1970.* Stanford, Calif.: Stanford University Press, 1998.

FEMINISM AND WOMEN'S LIBERATION

Baxandall, Rosalyn, and Linda Gordon, eds. *Dear Sisters: Dispatches from the Women's Liberation Movement.* New York: Basic Books, 2000.

Davis, Flora. *Moving the Mountain: The Women's Movement in America since 1960.* Urbana: University of Illinois Press, 1999.

Echols, Alice. *Daring to Be Bad: Radical Feminism in America, 1967–1975.* Minneapolis: University of Minnesota Press, 1989.

Evans, Sara. *Personal Politics: The Origins of Women's Liberation in the Civil Rights Movement and the New Left.* New York: Vintage, 1979.

Ezekiel, Judith. *Feminism in the Heartland.* Columbus: Ohio State University Press, 2002.

Freeman, Jo. *The Politics of Women's Liberation: A Case Study of an Emerging Social Movement and Its Relation to the Policy Process.* New York: McKay, 1975.

Harrison, Cynthia. *On Account of Sex: The Politics of Women's Issues, 1945–1968.* Berkeley: University of California Press, 1988.

Hartmann, Susan M. *The Other Feminists: Activists in the Liberal Establishment.* New Haven, Conn.: Yale University Press, 1998.

Horowitz, Daniel. *Betty Friedan and the Making of "The Feminine Mystique": The American Left, the Cold War, and Modern Feminism.* Amherst: University of Massachusetts Press, 1998.

Meyerowitz, Joanne, ed. *Not June Cleaver: Women and Gender in Postwar America, 1945–1960.* Philadelphia: Temple University Press, 1994.

Rosen, Ruth. *The World Split Open: How the Modern Women's Movement Changed America.* New York: Viking, 2000.

Rupp, Leila J., and Verta Taylor. *Survival in the Doldrums: The American Women's Rights Movement, 1945 to the 1960s.* Columbus: Ohio State University Press, 1990.

Weigand, Kate. *Red Feminism: American Communists and the Making of Women's Liberation.* Baltimore: Johns Hopkins University Press, 2001.

AMERICA'S THIRD WORLD: BROWN, RED, AND YELLOW POWER

Garcia, Ignacio M. *Chicanismo: The Forging of a Militant Ethos among Mexican Americans.* Tucson: University of Arizona Press, 1997.

Gomez-Quinones, Juan. *Chicano Politics: Reality and Promise, 1940–1990.* Albuquerque: University of New Mexico Press, 1990.

Josephy, Alvin M. Jr., Joane Nagel, and Troy Johnson. *Red Power: The American Indians' Fight for Freedom.* 2nd ed. Lincoln: University of Nebraska Press, 1999.

Louie, Steve, and Glenn Omatsu. *Asian Americans: The Movement and the Moment.* Los Angeles: UCLA Asian American Studies Center Press, 2001.

Munoz, Carlos Jr. *Youth, Identity, Power: The Chicano Movement.* London: Verso, 1989.

Smith, Paul Chatt, and Robert Allen Warrior. *Like a Hurricane: The Indian Movement from Alcatraz to Wounded Knee.* New York: New Press, 1996.

Torres, Andres, and Jose E. Velazquez. *The Puerto Rican Movement: Voices from the Diaspora.* Philadelphia: Temple University Press, 1998.

GAY LIBERATION AND GAY RIGHTS

Adam, Barry D. *The Rise of the Gay and Lesbian Movement.* Boston: Twayne, 1987.

Clendinen, Dudley, and Adam Nagourney. *Out for Good: The Struggle to Build a Gay Rights Movement in America.* New York: Simon and Schuster, 1999.

D'Emilio, John. *Sexual Politics, Sexual Communities: The Making of a Homosexual Minority in the United States, 1940–1970.* Chicago: University of Chicago Press, 1983.

Duberman, Martin. *Stonewall.* New York: Dutton, 1993.

Escoffier, Jeffrey. *American Homo: Community and Perversity.* Berkeley: University of California Press, 1998.

Stein, Marc. *City of Sisterly and Brotherly Loves: Lesbian and Gay Philadelphia, 1945–1972.* Chicago: University of Chicago Press, 2000.

Suran, Justin David. "Coming Out against the War: Antimilitarism and the Politicization of Homosexuality in the Era of Vietnam," *American Quarterly,* 55, no. 3 (2001): 452–88.

THE NEW LEFT'S LEGACY

Berman, Paul. *A Tale of Two Utopias: The Political Journey of the Generation of 1968.* New York: W. W. Norton, 1996.

Edsall, Thomas Byrne, and Mary Edsall. *Chain Reaction: The Impact of Race, Rights, and Taxes on American Politics.* New York: W. W. Norton, 1991.

Epstein, Barbara. *Political Protest and Cultural Revolution: Nonviolent Direct Action in the 1970s and 1980s.* Berkeley: University of California Press, 1991.

Gosse, Van, and Richard Moser. *The World the Sixties Made: Politics and Culture since the 1960s.* Philadelphia: Temple University Press, 2003.

BIOGRAPHIES AND MEMOIRS

Baraka, Amiri. *The Autobiography of LeRoi Jones.* Chicago: Lawrence Hill Books, 1997.

Boggs, Grace Lee. *Living for Change: An Autobiography.* Minneapolis: University of Minnesota Press, 1998.

Branch, Taylor. *Parting the Waters: America in the King Years, 1954–63.* New York: Simon and Schuster, 1988.

———. *Pillar of Fire: America in the King Years, 1963–65.* New York: Simon and Schuster, 1998.

Brown, Elaine. *A Taste of Power: A Black Woman's Story.* New York: Pantheon, 1992.

Brownmiller, Susan. *In Our Time: Memoir of a Revolution.* New York: Dial Press, 1999.

Carew, Jan. *Ghosts in Our Blood: With Malcolm X in Africa, England, and the Caribbean.* Chicago: Lawrence Hill, 1994.

Fleming, Cynthia Griggs. *Soon We Will Not Cry: The Liberation of Ruby Doris Smith Robinson.* Lanham, Md.: Rowman and Littlefield, 1998.

Forman, James. *The Making of Black Revolutionaries.* New York: Macmillan, 1972.

Garrow, David J. *Bearing the Cross: Martin Luther King, Jr., and the Southern Christian Leadership Conference.* New York: Random House, 1986.

Halstead, Fred. *Out Now! A Participant's Account of the American Movement against the Vietnam War.* New York: Pathfinder, 1978.

Hayden, Tom. *Reunion: A Memoir.* New York: Random House, 1988.

Hilliard, David, and Lewis Cole. *This Side of Glory: The Autobiography of David Hilliard and the Story of the Black Panther Party.* Boston: Little, Brown, 1993.

Jay, Karla. *Tales of the Lavender Menace: A Memoir of Liberation.* New York: Basic Books, 1999.

Lee, Chana Kai. *For Freedom's Sake: The Life of Fannie Lou Hamer.* Urbana: University of Illinois Press, 1999.

Lipsitz, George. *A Life in the Struggle: Ivory Perry and the Culture of Opposition.* Philadelphia: Temple University Press, 1995.

Ransby, Barbara. *Ella Baker and the Black Freedom Movement: A Radical Democratic Vision.* Chapel Hill: University of North Carolina Press, 2003.

Robinson, Jo Ann Ooiman. *Abraham Went Out: A Biography of A. J. Muste.* Philadelphia: Temple University Press, 1981.

Strickland, William. *Malcolm X: Make It Plain.* New York: Penguin, 1994.

Timmons, Stuart. *The Trouble with Harry Hay: Founder of the Modern Gay Movement.* Boston: Alyson, 1990.

Tyson, Timothy B. *Radio Free Dixie: Robert F. Williams and the Roots of Black Power.* Chapel Hill: University of North Carolina Press, 1999.

Weiss, Nancy J. *Whitney M. Young, Jr., and the Struggle for Civil Rights.* Princeton, N.J.: Princeton University Press, 1989.

Woodard, Komozi. *A Nation within a Nation: Amiri Baraka (LeRoi Jones) and Black Power Politics.* Chapel Hill: University of North Carolina Press, 1999.

ACKNOWLEDGMENTS

Sally Belfrage, excerpt from *Freedom Summer* (Charlottesville: University of Virginia Press, 1990). Copyright © 1965 by Sally Belfrage. Reprinted with the permission of the Irene Skolnick Literary Agency.

Daniel Berrigan, excerpt from *Night Flight to Hanoi: War Diary with 11 Poems* (New York: Macmillan Publishing Company, 1968). Copyright © 1968 by Daniel Berrigan. Reprinted with the permission of the author.

Black Panther Party, "The Ten-Point Program: What We Want/What We Believe" (October 1966), from *The Black Panthers Speak: The Manifesto of the Party: The First Complete Documentary Record of the Panthers' Program,* edited by Philip S. Foner. Copyright © 1970 by Philip S. Foner. Reprinted with the permission of HarperCollins Publishers, Inc.

Boston Women's Health Book Collective, excerpt from *Our Bodies, Ourselves.* Copyright © 1971, 1973 by The Boston Women's Health Collective, Inc. Reprinted with the permission of Simon & Schuster Adult Publishing Group.

Stokely Carmichael and Charles V. Hamilton, excerpt from *Black Power: The Politics of Liberation in America.* Copyright © 1967 by Stokely Carmichael and Charles V. Hamilton. Reprinted with the permission of Random House, Inc.

Betty Friedan, excerpt from *The Feminine Mystique.* Copyright © 1963 by Betty Friedan. Reprinted with the permission of W. W. Norton & Company, Inc.

Tom Grace, "Remembering the Killings at Kent State" from *From Camelot to Kent State,* edited by Joan Morrison and Robert K. Morrison. Copyright © 1987 by Joan Morrison and Robert K. Morrison. Reprinted with the permission of John A. Ware Literary Agency. Currently available in paperback from Oxford University Press.

Fannie Lou Hamer, "Remembering 1962" from Howell Raines, *My Soul Is Rested: Movement Days in the Deep South Remembered.* Copyright © 1977 by Howell Raines. Reprinted with the permission of G. P. Putnam's Sons, a division of Penguin Group (USA) Inc.

Casey Hayden and Mary King, "Sex and Caste" (November 18, 1965). Reprinted with the permission of the authors.

Tom Hayden and the Students for a Democratic Society, excerpt from "The Port Huron Statement" (August 1962). Reprinted with the permission of Tom Hayden.

Maulana Karenga, "Nguzo Saba (The Seven Principles)" (1967), from www .officialkwanzaawebsite.org/NguzoSaba.html. Reprinted with the permission of Dr. Maulana Karenga.

Dr. Martin Luther King, Jr., "Letter from Birmingham Jail" (April 16, 1963). Copyright © 1963 by Martin Luther King, Jr.; copyright renewed 1991 by Coretta Scott King. "Declaration of Independence from the War in Vietnam" (Riverside Church, New York, April 4, 1967) from Clayborne Carson and Kris Shepard, eds., *A Call to Conscience: The Landmark Speeches of Dr. Martin Luther King, Jr.* (New York: IPM/Warner Books, 2001). Copyright © 1967 by Martin Luther King, Jr.; copyright renewed 1996 by Coretta Scott King. Both reprinted with the permission of The Heirs to the Estate of Martin Luther King, Jr., c/o Writer's House, Inc., as agent for the proprietor.

Mike Klonsky, excerpt from "Toward a Revolutionary Youth Movement" from *New Left Notes* (December 23, 1968). Reprinted with the permission of the author.

Hilda Sidney Krech, excerpt from "The Identity of Modern Woman" from *The Nation* (Centennial issue, September 20, 1965). For subscription information, call 1-800-333-8536. Portions of each week's *Nation* magazine can be accessed at http://www.thenation.com.

John Lewis, "Wake Up America!" (speech at the March on Washington, August 28, 1963). Reprinted with the permission of The Honorable John Lewis.

Jo Ann Gibson Robinson, letter to Mayor W. A. Gayle, Montgomery, Alabama (May 21, 1954) from *The Montgomery Bus Boycott and the Women Who Started It: The Memoir of Jo Ann Gibson Robinson,* edited by David J. Garrow. Copyright © 1987 by the University of Tennessee Press. Reprinted with the permission of the publishers.

Mario Savio, excerpt from "An End to History" (speech at University of California at Berkeley, November 1964). Reprinted with the permission of Lynne Hollander Savio.

Malcolm X, excerpt from "Message to the Grassroots" (speech to the Northern Negro Grassroots Leadership Conference, November 10, 1963). Copyright © 1965, 1989 by Betty Shabazz and Pathfinder Press. Reprinted with permission.

Index

193

pan-Indian identity, 27
Parks, Rosa, 6, 44
  "Montgomery Bus Boycott, The: Talk at
    the Highlander School," 46–48
participatory democracy, 12, 67
passive resistance, 3. *See also* civil disobedi-
    ence
patriarchy, 14
peace movement. *See* antiwar activism
peers, trial by, 105
Peru, 118
Pine Ridge Reservation, South Dakota, 27,
    179
"Plan de Santa Barbara, El" (Movimiento
    Estudiantil Chicano de Aztlán), 142–45
Planned Parenthood, 69
police brutality, 105
police harassment, 151–53
political prisoners, 136
"Politics of the Strike, The" (Third World
    Liberation Front), 127–28
"Port Huron Statement, The" (Hayden/Stu-
    dents for a Democratic Society), 12,
    65–67, 176
"Position Paper (Women in the Move-
    ment)", 21
Potter, Paul
  "Incredible War, The," 95–99
poverty programs, 115, 121
Powell, Adam Clayton, 171*n*
Powers, Francis Gary, 58*n*
"Preamble to Constitution" (Gay Activists
    Alliance), 149–50
President's Commission on the Status of
    Women, 15, 109
"Principles" (New York Radical Women),
    123–24
prisoners of war, 136
"Proclamation" (Indians of All Tribes),
    145–48
Progressive Party, 42
PSP. *See* Puerto Rican Socialist Party (PSP)
Puerto Rican Revolutionary Workers Orga-
    nization, 134
Puerto Ricans
  culture of, 136
  organization of, 29
  self-determination for, 134–37
Puerto Rican Socialist Party (PSP), 29

racial discrimination
  against African Americans, 78–80
  against Chicanos, 143
"radical feminism," 21. *See also* feminism
Radical Feminists, 123
radicalism, principles of, 2, 49–51
radical lesbians, 30
radical liberalism, 24, 35
Raza Unida Party (United Race), 28
Reagan, Ronald, 35

Red Power movement, 27
Red Scare, 2, 4, 5, 14, 38, 41–42
Redstockings, 123
Reeb, James, 91*n*
"Remembering Freedom Summer" (Bel-
    frage), 84–86
"Remembering 1962" (Hamer), 61–64
"Remembering the Killings at Kent State"
    (Grace), 156–60
renacimiento, 142
Republican Party, conservatives, 5, 35
Reserve Officers Training Corps (ROTC),
    57
Resistance (anti-draft network), 17, 177
  "We Refuse—October 16," 112–13
Revolutionary Youth Movement, 23, 129
Rhodes, James, 156
Riggs, Jim, 157
Robinson, Jo Ann
  "Letter to Mayor W. A. Gayle," 44–45
Roe v. Wade, 31, 179
Roosevelt, Eleanor, 5, 52
Roosevelt, Franklin Delano, 5
ROTC. *See* Reserve Officers Training Corps
    (ROTC)
Rubin, Jerry, 22
Rusk, Dean, 98
Rustin, Bayard, 49

Sams, George, 153
SANE. *See* Committee for a Sane Nuclear
    Policy (SANE)
San Francisco, Calif.
  American Legion Convention, 58
  Free Speech Movement and, 12–13
  gay and lesbian rights movement, 15–16
  North Beach, 57
San Francisco State University, 26, 127,
    145
Santo Domingo (Dominican Republic),
    135
Sarachild, Kathie, 123
  "Outline for Consciousness-Raising,"
    154–55
Savio, Mario, 13
  "End to History, An," 87–90
Scheuer, Sandy, 159, 160
Schlesinger, Arthur, Jr., 5
Schroeder, Bill, 160
Schwerner, Rita, 86
SCLC. *See* Southern Christian Leadership
    Conference (SCLC)
SDS. *See* Students for a Democratic Society
    (SDS)
Seale, Bobby, 19, 26, 103–4
Second Congress to United Women, 30
Second Sex, The (Beauvoir), 71
segregation
  bills outlawing, 11
  civil disobedience and, 73–75